"Franklin always has so many incredible insights to share. This is another reader-friendly work that promises to plant a seed of change. It is DEFINITELY time for change!"

— **Dr. Marie Sobers**, Internship Supervisor, George Mason University; Presenter and Advocate for Non-traditional Education

"Franklin does a great job in using statistics and research data! Very detailed and interesting. As always, he amazes me with his knowledge and talent for writing."

— **Dr. Melinda Strickland**, Floyd County, Georgia Board of Education Member

"Franklin Schargel is a career educator who provides a text that should be at your fingertips or on your nightstand. Franklin points out the core of effective schools is the staff, not the programs. He skillfully weaves research-based suggestions with practical wisdom in an extremely accessible book. There are no magic bullets, no secrets to bumping up scores. It's hard work by a school team and, time and time again, Schargel reminds us that it is 'us and not me.'"

— **Peter Goodman**, Author of *Ed in the Apple Blog*

P9-APQ-427

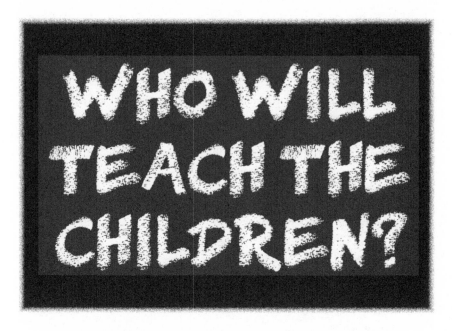

WHO WILL TEACH THE CHILDREN?

Recruiting, Retaining & Refreshing
Highly Effective Educators

FRANKLIN P. SCHARGEL

School Success Network Press

Published by School Success Network Press.
For more information, visit www.schargel.com

ISBN: 978-1-7334131-0-7   (print)
ISBN: 978-1-7334131-1-4   (ebook)

Editor: Richard Slovak
Designer: Deana Riddle
Cover Illustration: Howard Schargel

Portions of Chapter 3 previously appeared in Franklin Schargel, Tony Thacker, and John S. Bell, *From At-Risk to Academic Excellence: What Successful Leaders Do* (Larchmont, N.Y.: Eye on Education, 2007). Portions of Chapters 3 and 4 previously appeared in Tony Thacker, John S. Bell, and Franklin Schargel, *Creating School Cultures That Embrace Learning: What Successful Leaders Do* (Larchmont, N.Y.: Eye on Education, 2009), or in Franklin Schargel, *Dropout Prevention Tools* (Larchmont, N.Y.: Eye on Education, 2003).

Printed in the United States of America

To Dr. Myron Tribus
(October 30, 1921–August 31, 2016)

Quality Guru
Mentor
Friend

"Remembering that I'll be dead soon is the most important tool I've ever encountered to help me make the big choices in life. Because almost everything—all external expectations, all pride, all fear of embarrassment or failure—these things just fall away in the face of death, leaving only what is truly important. . . . Being the richest man in the cemetery doesn't matter to me. Going to bed at night saying we've done something wonderful . . . that's what matters to me."

—Steve Jobs

New
Teachers

New
Administrators

Lack of Support
Low Salaries
Burn-Out
Lack of Public Support
Lack of Resources
Poor Communication

*Teachers Leaving
Profession*

*Administrator
Quality*

Concept developed by Dr.Tony Thacker
Assistant State Superintendent of Education - State of Alabama

CONTENTS

FOREWORD

Dr. Sandy Addis, Director, National Dropout Prevention Center   1

INTRODUCTION   3

PART I: RECRUITING

Chapter 1: Interviewing / Hiring   21

PART II: RETAINING

Chapter 2: High-Performing Classrooms: Where Quality Shows   29

Chapter 3: Leadership: The Backbone of School Improvement   39

Chapter 4: School Culture   81

PART III: REFRESHING

Chapter 5: Refreshing the Current Staff   99

Chapter 6: Additional Strategies to Slow the Education Exodus   105

Chapter 7: Creating a Globally Competitive, World-Class School System   125

CONCLUSION

"The Bridge Builder"   138

Resources   141

Acknowledgments   151

About Franklin Schargel   153

FOREWORD

"Who will teach our children?" is one of the most important yet under-considered questions in education today. Teachers, who control classroom climate, instructional relevance, and student engagement, are held responsible for preventing student dropouts, yet nationally they have an early career dropout rate higher than that of their students. As with student dropouts, the causes of teacher dropouts are many, varied, complex, and challenging. Like student risk factors, the influences and forces that are correlated with early career exit of teachers not only are found in the school system but also are rooted in the economy, the community, the family, and the individual educator's preparation and value system.

Like the effective strategies that prevent student dropouts, keeping effective educators in the classroom is likely to be accomplished not by random acts of teacher retention but instead by strategies that address root causes, engage numerous stakeholders, change systems, and alter cultures and climates. Franklin Schargel, a veteran educator and leading authority in student dropout prevention for decades, is uniquely able to frame, address, and guide us toward answers to this critical question.

Dr. Sandy Addis
Director, National Dropout Prevention Center

INTRODUCTION

The United States faces a serious educational crisis. Teachers are leaving the classroom almost as quickly as colleges and universities prepare them. Many people are unaware that the teacher and administrator "dropout rate" is significantly higher than the student dropout rate. Research indicates that while about 18 percent of students fail to graduate from high school, close to 50 percent of teachers leave within five years, including 17 percent of first-year teachers (as described in a *Washington Post* article and by the National Education Association and the National Center for Education Statistics). The *Wall Street Journal* reported at the end of 2018, using U.S. Department of Labor figures, that teachers are quitting their jobs at record rates, since such records began to be kept in 2001: in the first ten months of 2018, public educators quit at an average rate of 83 per 10,000 on staff.

Why are teachers, and others in the field, leaving? What grade levels are most affected? What subjects are losing the most educators? Are certain geographic areas affected more than others? At what experiential levels are they leaving? In addition to educational disruption, what are the costs to school systems? What can be done to stop the hemorrhaging of these trained and certified educators? The overriding question is, who will teach the children?

I am a lifelong professional educator, but we are a disappearing breed. Many of those trained to become educators never enter the classroom. Blame it on the long hours, low salaries, lack of training on how to handle disruptive students, insufficient administrative support, and the figurative microscope through which the media and public examine educators and blame them when schools are deemed "low performing."

I will never forget the first day of my teaching career. After filling out the required paperwork, I was taken by the assistant principal for administration on a brief tour of the building. The assistant principal pointed out the teachers' lounge, the male teachers' bathrooms, and my classroom. He handed me a roll book and the keys to my classroom and then wished me good luck. I thought, as he did, that my college had prepared me for any eventuality. I had graduated and was convinced that my professors had transmitted all the knowledge and training that they possessed, giving me the skills I needed to thrive in the educational system. I felt certain that all I had to do was to use the techniques I had been taught.

In fact, my college professors were interested in teaching me a great deal of theory but little that I could use in a classroom. So when I graduated, I had only a bit more practical knowledge than when I had started. My first assignment, a high school, was in the Harlem section of New York. What did a young white male know about the economically challenged minority students I was about to meet? What did my instructors at the City University of New York know about the culture of the school? It did not take me long to learn that if I wanted to succeed as an educator, I would have to learn on the job.

Unfortunately, my experience is not unique. I want to share what I have learned over time. Teachers today are inadequately trained or prepared for the students, parents, and conditions they face. What I have learned has come from personal experience—over time and by reading and listening to others in the field. I estimate that I have delivered more than 250 workshops to over 50,000 educators. I ask at each workshop, "How many of you were well prepared to enter the classroom when you graduated from your school of education?" The clear majority say they were not. And the problem has grown worse as schools and teachers are forced to deal with an increasing number of nontraditional students (minority, impoverished, foster, homeless, autistic) who come from nontraditional homes (single parent, divorce, second or third marriage) and learn in nontraditional ways (via the internet, tablets, social media).

Schools of education are reporting a steep decrease in student enrollment. Large states have been particularly hard hit, raising concerns about the supply of new teachers. For example, as reported in *Education Week*, California lost 53 percent of its school of education enrollment between the 2008–2009 and 2012–2013 school years.

It is not simply an American problem. The demand for skilled teachers around the world is large and growing. A recent study by the American

4

Association for Employment in Education found teacher shortages in at least half of the fields surveyed. UNESCO reported that the market for preprimary, primary, and secondary education worldwide expanded by more than 142 million students between 1999 and 2006. The growth in the number of students has resulted in demand for an additional 7.7 million trained teachers. In the United Kingdom, the *Daily Mail* reported that "almost three out of four local education authorities [LEAs] in England is experiencing a teacher shortage . . . and 18 per cent of those polled said the problem had reached crisis levels. . . . The poll for PA News also found some signs of a shortage in Scotland and Wales. . . . Of the 73 per cent of English LEAs surveyed that said their schools were struggling to find suitably qualified staff, half said the shortage was either moderate or severe," with math and modern language being "hardest to find."

Compounding the teacher shortage problem is the number of teachers departing. The Australian Broadcasting Corporation (ABC News) reported that the number of teachers leaving the profession in recent years had increased, prompting concern that Australia could be facing a teacher shortage similar to those in the United States and the United Kingdom. The Australian National University researched teacher attrition rates and found that the level of work teachers are expected to do has increased over time, causing teachers to "burn out." Time pressures and lack of administrative support were having a harmful effect on the teaching profession, according to an Australian Senate "Teaching and Learning" Inquiry in 2013. While the causes may differ from place to place, the result is essentially the same: the teaching profession has suffered major challenges across the globe.

This is certainly an American problem as well. For example, the Arizona Department of Education has compiled data showing that thousands of teachers have left schools in the past five years. A department task force's report estimated that seventy-two thousand employees left the Arizona State Retirement System before reaching retirement. The department also reported the annual teacher retention rate at only 65 percent. Arizona superintendents attributed the mass exodus to low pay and no raises.

Nationwide, a conservative estimate of the cost of replacing public school teachers who have dropped out of the profession is $2.2 billion a year, according to *Teacher Attrition*, a report from the Alliance for Excellent Education. If the cost of replacing public school teachers who transfer from one school to another is added, the total reaches $4.9 billion every year. For individual states, those cost estimates range from $8.5 million in North Dakota to half a billion dollars in Texas. In the next decade, according to the U.S. Department of Education, the American Federation of Teachers, and the National Education Association, American schools will need more than 2 million new teachers.

Teachers are the most essential component in the learning process, and the large number of teachers retiring are taking with them their knowledge and expertise, exacerbating the situation by creating a gap in experience. It is not only the loss of warm bodies that should concern us, but also the difficulty of building an experienced base of teaching and learning techniques that the new, inexperienced, and weakly trained staff will need time to accumulate. Some states already faced with the problem are issuing emergency licenses—thereby weakening, rather than strengthening, the teaching cadre of their schools. Some administrators have had to hire teachers with little or no classroom experience, causing classroom management problems, not only for those newly hired but also for nearby classrooms and teachers. The No Child Left Behind Act of 2001, the federal legislation for standards-based education reform, gives parents the right to know the qualifications of their children's teachers and paraprofessionals. Far too many school districts face an uphill battle when it comes to recruiting and retaining highly effective teachers, especially those who serve students from low-income families. In fact, students in poor and minority schools are twice as likely to have an inexperienced teacher and are 61 percent more likely to be assigned an uncertified teacher. Consider the following:

- According to a report by Linda Darling-Hammond for the National Commission on Teaching and America's Future, "Every school day, nearly a thousand teachers leave the field of teaching. Another thousand teachers change schools, many in pursuit of better working conditions. And the figures do not include the teachers who retire."

- The same report states that the number is dramatically higher—roughly 50 percent—in hard-to-staff schools in inner cities and in minority neighborhoods where poverty rules.

- Among teachers who transferred between schools, lack of planning time (65 percent), too heavy a workload (60 percent), problematic student behavior (53 percent), and a lack of influence over school policy (52 percent) were cited by the U.S. Department of Education's National Center for Education Statistics as common sources of dissatisfaction.

- From the same study: "The current teachers' shortage represents arguably the most imminent threat to the nation's schools. The U.S. Department of Education estimates that approximately 2.2 million teachers will be needed over the next decade—an average of more than 200,000 new teachers annually."

- According to author Lynn F. Howard, what is perceived to be a teaching shortage is really a retention problem. In fact, teachers are leaving the field faster than colleges are preparing new ones.

- A report by Richard Ingersoll has observed that new teachers are particularly vulnerable because they are more likely than more experienced teachers to be assigned to low-performing schools in urban areas, where the dropout rates reach or exceed 50 percent. It is here that teachers need the most assistance, yet most new teachers are given little professional support or feedback, and few are provided with demonstrations of what it takes to help their students succeed.

- In an annual *MetLife Survey of the American Teacher*, new teachers reported being greatly stressed by administrative duties, classroom management, and testing responsibilities as well as by their relationships (or lack thereof) with parents.

- As described by authors Annette L. Breaux and Harry K. Wong, estimates of the proportion of new teachers in urban schools who will not finish even their first year as a teacher run as high as 9.3 to 17 percent. Between 40 and 50 percent will leave during the first seven years of their career, and more than two-thirds of those will do so in the first four years of teaching.

- We are losing the best and brightest. A study by the North Central Regional Educational Laboratory found that according to a majority of superintendents in the region, between 75 and 100 percent of the teachers who are leaving are "effective or "very effective" in the classroom. The authors, Debra Hare and James L. Heap, suggest that the most academically talented teachers leave in the greatest numbers.

- The loss of talented teachers is also significant in rural schools, which, in addition, face the problem of lower teacher salaries and the difficulty of recruiting new teachers.

- Why is teacher turnover so high? In one analysis of the subject, described by Richard Ingersoll, teachers reported that they left because of failure to receive the administrative support they expected.

- Students today are looking less and less like their teachers, as noted in an article by Lauren Camera in *U.S. News & World Report*. Most American teachers are white women, but the majority of K–12 students are from minority groups.

- In a report for the National Commission on Teaching and America's Future, Thomas Carroll and Elizabeth Foster wrote that 53 percent of today's teachers are baby boomers; in eighteen states, more than half of the teachers are already over age fifty; and in seventeen states, 45 percent of the teaching workforce is over age fifty.

A report by Public Agenda and Learning Point Associates, *Teaching for a Living: How Teachers See the Profession Today*, offers a comprehensive look at how teachers across the country differ in perspectives on their profession. Based on a nationwide survey asking nearly nine hundred teachers more than one hundred questions, this study revealed three broad categories representative of teachers nationwide. Researchers labeled these categories "Disheartened," "Contented," and "Idealists." One question asked respondents whether they agreed with the view that teaching is "so demanding, it's a wonder more people don't burn out"; this feeling is pervasive, particularly among the "Disheartened." This group, comprising 40 percent of the teachers surveyed, tends to have taught longer and be older than the Idealists. More than half teach in low-income schools. By contrast, teachers in the Contented group (37 percent of the teachers surveyed) viewed teaching as a lifelong career. These teachers tend to be veterans—94 percent have been teaching for more than ten years, most have graduate degrees, and about two-thirds teach in middle-income or affluent schools.

However, it is the Idealists (23 percent of the teachers surveyed) who voiced the strongest sense of mission about teaching. More than half are thirty-two or younger and teach in elementary schools, and 63 percent said that they intend to stay in education, while 36 percent of this group said they plan to leave classroom teaching for other jobs in the field. One might assume that teachers in public schools are those leaving the field, whereas charter school teachers, who voluntarily decided to teach at nontraditional charter schools, would be more likely to stay in teaching. But a study published by the National Center for the Study of Privatization in Education, at Teachers College, Columbia University, shows that for charter school teachers, the odds are 132 percent greater (compared with public school teachers) that a teacher will leave the profession rather than stay at the same school.

The study, by David Stuit and Thomas Smith, also says that charter school teachers are 76 percent more likely than public school teachers to switch schools than to stay at the same school. The research draws on national survey data for the 2003–2004 school year. The survey showed that 25 percent of charter school teachers turned over that year, compared to 14 percent of traditional public school teachers. Fourteen percent of the charter teachers left the profession altogether, and 11 percent moved to a different school. Among the public school teachers, 7 percent left the profession and 7 percent switched schools.

A follow-up study by the two authors for Vanderbilt University's National Center on Student Choice provides some additional calculations aimed at pinpointing the reasons why so many more charter teachers are leaving. Are they quitting in frustration or leaving involuntarily? Mostly the former, according to the researchers, who wrote that compared to traditional public school teachers, charter school teachers are more likely to voluntarily leave the profession or move to a new school because they are dissatisfied with the school and its working conditions. What has caused this problem of recruiting and retaining teachers? According to Arne Duncan, then U.S. secretary of education, part of the problem has been caused by the failure of America's colleges of education to adequately prepare future teachers for success. "By almost any standard, many if not most of the nation's 1,450 schools, colleges, and departments of education are doing a mediocre job of preparing teachers for the realities of the 21st century classroom," Duncan said in a speech at Columbia University.

More than half of the nation's teachers graduate from a school of education. The U.S. Department of Education estimates that 220,000 students, or 80 percent of incoming teachers, graduate from a teachers college every year. Noting then that America's schools would need to hire up to 200,000 first-time teachers annually for the next five years, Duncan said that those new teachers needed the knowledge and skills to prepare students for success in the global economy. The secretary's statements echoed the words of Arthur Levine, former president of Teachers College at Columbia University, who currently serves as president of the Woodrow Wilson National Fellowship Foundation. His report *Educating School Teachers*, released by the Education Schools Project, found that three of five alumni of education schools said their training had failed to prepare them to teach. "At the moment, teacher education is the Dodge City of the education world. Like the Wild West town, it is unruly and disordered." He added that there is a chasm between what goes on in the university and what goes on in the classroom. The report goes on to say that most teacher education programs are deeply flawed. The coursework in teacher education programs is in disarray nationwide. Unlike other professions such as law and medicine, there is no common length of study or set of required skills.

A study by the business school at the University of California, Los Angeles, showed that the U.S. Air Force has come to recognize that the cost, in terms of training and experience, of losing a pilot for any reason is $1,439,754. While the financial cost of training a teacher is certainly not the same, the loss of a teacher is also significant in terms of investment in training and experience. If we look at the business world, two of the most successful companies, Starbucks and Southwest Airlines, believe that their most important customers are their workers; if the employees enjoy working, they will make that company's ultimate customer happy. Other companies, such as Google, Apple, and Amazon, are replicating this philosophy. Can we in education—where the ultimate customers are the students, and their parents—come to recognize this as well? After all, students are temporary personnel, while classroom educators are supposedly "permanent parties." Can we, by making our frontline people happy, make our ultimate customers happy?

Teaching can be a frustrating job. Unlike the idealized image of students sitting patiently with their hands folded, waiting for knowledge to be poured into their heads, many of today's students come to class bringing with them enormous challenges. Children are expected to deal with divorce, drugs, violence, merged families, and parental neglect. They also show up in school with various abilities, capabilities, and needs. Many parents have made efforts to prepare the students for learning. In other cases, however, parents have done little; they have not taken the time or had the energy to train their children in some of the fundamentals such as studying, reading, learning the alphabet, even how to spell their name. School administrators need to understand these challenges and create school cultures that allow teachers to reach every child. This means teachers need to take chances that may not always succeed. In dealing with people, we do not expect every experiment to succeed. Doctors, like teachers, do not have 100 percent success. Teachers are becoming more frustrated than ever in dealing with the problems they face.

In the report *A Possible Dream: Retaining California Teachers So All Students Learn*, Ken Futernick identified numerous challenges to teachers:

- More and more children are coming to school without family support.

- Teachers are required to do more and more in a limited period of time.

- Teachers are expected to be experts in all fields.

- There is too little planning time.

- There is too much paperwork.

- Assistance from the district is unreliable.

- Administrative support is lacking.

- Teachers work weekends without pay.

- Teachers spend summer vacations taking college classes or preparing for the next school year.

- Teachers face undue pressure from students' parents.

- Students need more time and attention.

The report offered six recommendations for retaining teachers:

1. School administrators should continuously assess teaching conditions.

2. Education funding should be increased to at least adequate levels.

3. The state should introduce administrative policies that support teachers' instructional needs.

4. Principals should focus on "high-quality teaching and learning conditions."

5. The state should establish standards for teaching and learning conditions.

6. Administrators should address specific challenges in retaining special education teachers.

Clearly, something must be done to address the teacher dropout problem. This starts with the fact that schools of education are failing to adequately prepare teachers. As a result, the responsibility for ensuring well-prepared teachers rests with those in the field—through on-the-job training. When teachers graduate, they have a lot of book learning, but that does not make them competent to function as a quality educator. It is like reading every book on driving a car, taking a written test on driving, and then being put in the driver's seat of a car. They do not know how to practice teaching—only how to think about educational problems and answer test questions. Putting unskilled educators into classrooms, allowing them to make mistakes because of inexperience, puts students at risk. And, in fact, we give the least experienced, least trained educators the most difficult students to teach. Schools have become the nation's emergency room. Schools inherit the problems that society does not know how to address, or does not wish to: schools are expected to teach driving skills; how to say no to drugs, smoking, and sex; and how to avoid suicide. Educators have not been taught these skills; nor is there sufficient time in the day to teach these prevention skills.

Forty percent of the current public-school teaching force expect not to be teaching five years from now. According to an edition of the report *Profile of Teachers in the U.S.*, published by the National Center for Education Information, most teachers "teach primarily because they want to work with young people." But according to C. Emily Feistritzer, president of the center and coauthor of the report, that is changing, "with the rapidly aging population of teachers who are retiring at increasing rates and are increasingly being replaced by adults coming into teaching from other careers, who view education and teaching quite differently."

According to recent statistics, 50 percent of the 3.5 million public and private teachers in the United States were eligible to retire, and 260,000 had decided to leave the profession entirely (with a similar number taking another position in the field). We graduate 106,000 new education majors every year—but of that group, 40 percent will not work in the field of education. That leaves about 63,600 new teachers to fill 260,000 openings.

According to a report by William J. Hussar for the National Center for Education Statistics (NCES), projections for the number of newly hired public school teachers needed to replace retiring teachers over an eleven-year period ranged from 1.7 million to 2.7 million. Since 46 percent of all educators leave the field within five years, that means we need to hire between 2,482,000 and 3,942,000 new teachers within that time frame. Currently there are 3.7 million full-time elementary and secondary public school teachers engaged in classroom instruction. It used to be possible to fill these open positions with women who had recently graduated from college. Traditionally, the main occupations for women were secretaries, nurses, or teachers. But today women have greater job opportunities. Today, according to the NCES, 77 percent of all public school teachers are women and 56 percent of them are over the age of forty.

In Albuquerque, New Mexico, where I live, retirements are up 19 percent and resignations are up 13 percent over the previous year. According to Ellen Bernstein, president of the Albuquerque Teachers Federation, 575 teachers (out of 6,000) were removed from the union's rolls at the end of the 2015–2016 school year. Kim Burgess reported in the *Albuquerque Journal* that there were more than one hundred vacancies in schools, and librarians and assistant principals were asked to fill in for at least seventeen days as temporary teachers.

In the *Detroit Free Press*, Lori Higgins reported in 2017, "On any given day in the Detroit Public Schools Community District, about 100 classes are operating without a permanent teacher—the result of a dire teacher vacancy problem that is taxing schools, teachers, students and principals. As of April 27, the district had 263 teacher vacancies. Of that number, 161 were being filled by long-term substitute teachers, including several dozen that are part of a program that puts them on a quicker track toward full certification." The bump in retirements could not happen at a worse time, as districts are attempting to hire additional personnel to meet class size limits. The teachers who are leaving are taking with them their years of experience as well as the costs incurred by the district in training them.

Our K–12 teaching force is aging rapidly. The proportion of these teachers who are fifty or older rose from one in four (24 percent) in 1996 to 42 percent in 2005. The percentage of teacher in their thirties dropped from 37 percent in 1990 to 22 percent in 2005. The proportion of teachers in their forties has also dropped from 44 percent in 1996 to 26 percent in 2005. As a result, there is no longer a large cadre of the most experienced mentors available to train the newest members of the profession.

Educators who prepare teachers cannot know where prospective teachers will work and cannot prepare them for every setting, location, or grade level. This time-consuming work must be done in the school. It is difficult to train fledgling teachers to provide relevant materials and instructional techniques to their students. Teaching requires skills that are difficult to master. Teachers and administrators need training and support to meet the ever-changing challenges of the profession.

Education today is losing talent. Bright, capable young men and women are leaving teaching in sizable numbers, shifting their lives from the classrooms and the front offices into jobs that are less stressful, pay more, and are more appreciated. While the ebb and flow of young people into and out of the field of education is always a steady tide, the ongoing drain of experienced and bright young people after three, four, or five years is a concern.

As noted earlier, an Alliance for Excellent Education report states that teacher attrition costs the nation up to $2.2 billion a year. The national average teacher attrition rate is 16.5 percent. A report by Gary Barnes, Edward Crowe, and Benjamin Schaefer for the National Commission on Teachers and America's Future covered a number of school communities, including Jemez Valley, New Mexico, where on average the loss of a teacher cost the school district $4,366; Chicago, where the average cost was $17,872; and Milwaukee, where it was $15,325 per teacher—not including the cost in the disruption of learning in the schools.

Why do so many teachers leave the profession? In Albuquerque, in a study of teachers who left, 60 percent said the reasons included dissatisfaction with the job, 53 percent said they wanted a less stressful environment, 51 percent said their school was poorly managed, 46 percent said they did not like the state Public Education Department's use of tests to measure performance for teacher evaluations, 44 percent said they were overworked, and 42 percent said they were leaving for increased salaries.

Ongoing concerns about teacher shortages are not unique to the United States, and studies in other countries produce results that can be applicable here as well. In the United Kingdom, Sarah Marsh wrote in the *Guardian* about a report that explored the questions of why people become teachers and why so many stop. The survey of more than 1,000 teachers found that the vast majority (93%) joined the profession because they thought they would be good at it. And, Marsh wrote, "it seems the lightbulb moments keep teachers motivated—the main reason they stay is to make a difference (92%)." However, "researchers also uncovered considerable disillusionment, with 59% of respondents saying they had considered quitting in the past six months, mainly as a result of workload." To keep them from leaving, the report urged an emphasis on the positive impact the teachers were having on students, as well as the need to ensure that teachers are given manageable workloads. The study also debunked many stereotypes about teaching. Marsh wrote, "Pay and career progression, for example, were found to be less significant in terms of motivation than many might imagine."

The *Guardian* article used the findings of the report to examine a number of statements about teachers, asking the article's readers to judge which statements were based on fact and which were fiction:

1. Teachers join the profession because of the long holidays.

Only 17 percent cited the long summer break as a "very important" factor, and 35 percent said it was "fairly important." Conversely, almost all (93%) said they wanted to make a difference in students'

lives, and 60 percent cited this as a "very important" factor.
Verdict: fiction

2. **Teachers would recommend the job to their younger selves.**

   Perhaps surprisingly, even with teachers leaving in large numbers, more than half (52%) said they would still go into teaching if they could go back in time. One said, "I try to convince everybody to move into the profession, because you meet great people with big hearts. When I get on with people, the first thing I ask is why they don't work in a school."
   Verdict: fact

3. **But teachers would not recommend the job to their child or brightest student.**

   Although a majority do not regret joining the profession, only 34 percent would recommend it to their own child and only 41 percent to their brightest student. One crucial reason is how demanding the job can be. One teacher said, "Teaching is such a stressful job, it encompasses your life completely."
   Verdict: fact

4. **Poor behavior is the main reason teachers quit.**

   Despite a common image of a teacher driven to distraction by misbehaving students, researchers found behavior to be an issue for only 27 percent of those who had even considered leaving; concerns about workload (76%) and unhappiness with the quality of leadership (43%) were far more pressing.
   Verdict: fiction

5. **Pay is a major problem.**

   Only 43 percent of those who had thought about leaving felt the salary was insufficient, though 30 percent of those surveyed felt that pay was increasingly important as they

got older. Pay was also considered a minor reason to go into teaching in the first place—only 9 percent said it was "very important" and 39 percent found it "fairly important."
Verdict: fiction

6. Subject passion drives arts and humanities teachers most.

According to the survey, teachers of music (81%), history (86%), and modern foreign languages (76%) are more likely to have entered the profession because of a love for their subject than, for example, science teachers (63%). A possible reason for this is that there are more opportunities to work directly in science, technology, engineering, and math rather than teach those subjects, but fewer options outside of teaching in the humanities and arts.
Verdict: fact

7. Most teachers are not hoping for a lifelong career.

There is a widespread belief that many people fall into teaching but always planned to move to another profession later on. However, only 13 percent of those who had considered leaving said they had never thought of teaching as a permanent career.
Verdict: fiction

In this book, I share what I have discovered in my thirty-three years in schools, as well as words of wisdom from some of the most creative and innovative educators whom I have had the privilege of working with. The purpose of this book is make suggestions for new and experienced teachers and administrators and provide them with information to avoid the pitfalls faced by earlier generations of educators. This experience can help educators better communicate with parents and students.

PART I
RECRUITING

CHAPTER 1
Interviewing / Hiring

"It doesn't make sense to hire smart people and then tell them what to do; we hire smart people so they can tell us what to do."

—**Steve Jobs** in Shahrzad Rafati, *"What Steve Jobs Taught Executives about Hiring"*

Research indicates that the quality of students' learning is directly correlated with the quality of the teachers they have had. New teachers may have a lot of book learning from their school of education or college, but they do not yet know how to practice the profession of teaching (unless they have had experience in student teaching). Unskilled, inexperienced educators in classrooms put students at risk, and this is compounded by the fact that students with the greatest challenges are usually given teachers with the least amount of training and experience.

A majority of the thousands of educators taking part in the hundreds of workshops I have delivered during my career say they were not well prepared to enter the classroom after they graduated from their school of education. And principals agree with teachers: *Educating School Leaders*, a report by Arthur Levine, then the longtime president of Teachers College at Columbia University, cited a survey in which 89 percent of principals agreed that "schools of education do not adequately prepare their graduates to cope with classroom realities." If we want new people to thrive in the educational environment, we must be prepared to give them on-the-job training. And it is critical that educational systems start out by hiring the best of the best.

Interviewing

Schools need to develop a laser-like concentrated effort to find and hire highly qualified and highly effective individuals to teach. In my workshops,

I use a clip from the film *Ferris Bueller's Day Off*. The teacher played by Ben Stein is highly qualified but not highly effective. What is the difference? A highly qualified person knows what to teach, but not how to teach. It is essential to identify and hire not just highly qualified but also highly effective staff.

Have you ever had a teacher who knew all the material but could not teach? We all have. On the other hand, think of a teacher who made a positive difference in your life. Did he graduate from an Ivy League college? Maybe. Did she have a 4.0 GPA? Maybe. What qualities did they possess? We need to identify these qualities before we hire anyone, not after. We need to do a better job of hiring on the front end, rather than on the back end by letting them go.

Interviewing Questions. Before hiring someone, it is a good idea to develop a series of questions that you might ask applicants. Here are some possible questions:

- What is your definition of a good teacher?
- Why did you want to become a teacher?
- Who was your favorite teacher? Why?
- What would you like to accomplish?
- What are your strengths?
- What have you read lately?
- What do you like to do for fun?
- What is the greatest obstacle you have faced? How did you deal with it?
- What is the role of technology in the classroom?
- How would you interact with parents?
- How would you modify your lesson plans to deal with gifted students? Slow students?
- Do you like children? How would I know that, when I observed your class?

- What do you bring to the table to help the school achieve its mission?

- What would it mean to have a job that you love?

- How do you deal with things that are beyond your control? (In special education, rules must be followed.)

- How would you deal with a student in your class who had his head down? Who was sleeping? Who disrupted your class?

- What would you do if your lesson plan was not working?

- Where would you like to be in three years?

- What should I know about you that I have not asked?

- What have you done in the past three years that has not gone well? What did you do about it?

- What have you failed at?

Create an Interview Team. Broaden the circle when interviewing. Ask other teachers and anyone else who would be working with the person, if hired, to sit in on the interview. If you lack specific expertise, for example in special education or a foreign language, ask somebody from the district office or a neighboring school to sit in. Ask the school's union leader (if there is one) to join the interview process. Get input from all of these people before the interview. Have them contribute questions to ask. Find out if any of them would be willing to serve as mentors for the new hire.

In addition, teachers should be able to pass the tests that students are required to take. When I interviewed teachers, I asked them to take the tests that I expected students to pass (such as the New York State Regents Examination), after giving them time to study.

Who Makes the Most Effective Teachers?

Hire the best people you can find. Hiring is about trying to understand how the individual is going to fit in and what contributions he or she can make to improve the culture of the school. Hire people who have different skills from yours. Try to find people who are smarter than you are and have different viewpoints. Try to hire people who can improve the school and the district and will make the school team stronger. You need to create a culture where people want to be at work. If possible, never hurry when you are hiring. You have to be clear about what you want and what your expectations are. When you are clear, everyone understands. When you have an open position, do not hire someone who lacks the right skill set. Wait for the right person. Hiring should be more than a gut feeling. Look for people you want to spend time with and who have energy, passion, and a sense of what they want to accomplish. When hiring, focus on a person's potential more than on performance. We get so used to seeing a person in a certain role that we judge the person on performance in that role and not on his or her potential. You need to trust the people you hire, and they need to trust you. Trust is that important. And it needs to be trust by actions, not words.

Who makes the best teachers? As you interview, look for the following qualities of a highly effective teacher, which I have gathered over time based on what could be considered the qualities of the best teachers I, and colleagues of mine, have ever had. This list is in no way intended to be comprehensive. Nor is it in any particular order of importance. Some of this material is drawn from *Schools Where Teachers Lead: What Successful Leaders Do*, which John S. Bell, Tony Thacker, and I coauthored.

- Possesses a passion for both teaching and learning.
- Loves children. I used to ask, "Convince me that you love children." Any answer would be acceptable. I can teach you to teach, but I cannot teach you to love children.
- Is energetic.
- Recognizes that each child learns differently. Great teachers adjust their teaching levels to accommodate each student.
- Is innovative—effective teachers are willing to try new methods to improve instruction.
- Uses new tools and techniques—and is willing to abandon them if they do not work.

- Is optimistic—always sees a positive outcome. Never puts down students or peers.

- Develops a relationship with their students. Great teachers are always willing to make time for students, listen to them, and help when there is a problem.

- Builds relationships with parents as well as with students.

- Is a team player—collaborates with colleagues, families, and students to build academic achievement.

- Is willing to go beyond the expectations of others.

- Maintains good instructional skills—and has a desire to upgrade skills, taking in-service courses to stay ahead of the learning curve.

- Is a lifelong learner.

- Uses data to make informed decisions.

- Inspires others to achieve their potential.

- Has consistently high expectations for *all* students.

- Recognizes and adapts when not getting through to students.

- Has flexibility—is willing to abandon lessons if they are not working.

- Provides time to students, parents, and the community.

- Knows how to balance school, work, and personal family.

- Has the ability to build positive relationships.

- Uses twenty-first-century classroom learning tools, including the latest technology.

- Shows appreciation and enthusiasm for cultural differences.

- Inspires others to achieve their potential.

- Understands the complexity of teaching.

- Is a member of the mentoring team, giving back to colleagues and the school.

- Has the ability to communicate well.

- Is dedicated to teaching. Great teachers see education as a lifelong calling.

Once You Have Hired

The best advice you can give to a new teacher is this: "You are going to have good days and bad ones. Do not let the highs get you too high and the lows get you too low. There will be days when you are just exuberant over a big win of some kind, and then there are some days when nothing goes right. Try to stay grounded and surround yourself with people you can believe in—and then just get out there and do your best." Teachers may be under assault from students, parents, the administration, the board of education, and the media, but they need to avoid seeing themselves as victims.

To ease the entry of new teachers into the school and make them more comfortable, hang photos of them in the teachers' lunchroom. If you see the teacher in the hall, ask how things are going. Ask him or her to have lunch with you. Irving Anker, my first principal, asked all new teachers to meet with him during a common lunch period and said, "I am your rating officer. But I also want to help you succeed. Your failure would be my failure, so let's discuss how I can help you succeed."

Form an Observation Team. One way to find out if someone is qualified to be a teacher is to observe that person teaching a class. After an appropriate amount of time has passed, visit the new teacher's classroom. Let the team (composed of one or more colleagues as well as administrators) observe a lesson that a new hire teaches. The best predictor of a new teacher's success is classroom performance.

Newly hired teachers are stepping into a new setting and possibly a new culture. Help them adjust to the new environment. Give transparent feedback. Set transparent goals. Allow three to four months for the teacher to settle in before making judgments about retaining the person or letting him or her go. If all goes well, a new, inexperienced hire might just start to take the first steps toward becoming a great teacher.

PART II
RETAINING

CHAPTER 2

High-Performing Classrooms: Where Quality Shows

No School Can Outperform the Educators Inside It

New teachers come to their jobs with enthusiasm and idealistic views. But they are sometimes thrown into classrooms by administrators with a "sink or swim" mentality. New teachers lack practical skills. With an emphasis on the theoretical in the training they received in college, they lack the practical aspects of being a teacher. It may be difficult for new teachers to accomplish the most basic school chores without having to spend an inordinate amount of time and effort. Adding to the problem, we give the least experienced, least classroom-trained teachers the most difficult students to teach—part of the reason for our nation's high educator turnover rate. Classroom management is about their day-to-day survival. And frequently, we do not supply new teachers with mentors. They often ask, "Whom do I turn to for help?"

Teachers should be provided with help, and they should be coachable. I have heard students say, "I really worked hard," and I have had to reply, "But you didn't pass." Similarly, teachers should be able to defend any decision they make, providing good reasons for it. Give them feedback and see how they react to it. Either they are learning or they are arguing with you. Are they "yessing" you because they think that is what you want to hear?

As described in detail in a report by both the National Comprehensive Center for Teacher Quality and Public Agenda, teachers who come to the profession through "alternative routes"—newer programs that serve as options other than traditional schools of education—are especially motivated by the desire to help disadvantaged children, but at the same time they are more disheartened by the conditions they find in the classroom.

Among the questions new teachers should ask themselves are these:

- How can we make examinations be a way of checking knowledge transfer rather than a means of knowledge retrieval?
- How can we connect the education received in the classroom with real-environment conditions and competences?

Teachers need to meet students where they are and understand what motivates them.

One of my favorite tools was to use the "Cause and Effect Diagram." Start with the effect and work backward to reach the causes. I believe that teachers can use this (with all age groups) to draw students into conversations about studying, testing, and homework. Ask teachers to develop their own questions. I would ask the students, for example, "Why don't students do homework?" Or I would ask them why students did not study, including for tests. At teacher-parent meetings, I would ask the parents why other parents did not attend those meetings. The follow-up question could be, "What can we do about this?"

Encourage new teachers to ask for help when they hit a roadblock. Many of them feel embarrassed about not knowing what to do. Assure them that there is no shame in not knowing all the answers or in asking for help.

Education is a solitary profession. Lesson plans are generally developed and used by an individual teacher. Lessons are delivered in classrooms by an individual. Tests are generally created by a single person. Students are encouraged to study and work alone. But in the outside world, work is increasingly done thorough collaboration and teamwork. Students should be encouraged to work on teams—as should teachers. Lesson plans, curricula, and tests should be developed through collaboration. Teachers should be encouraged to observe one another and ask themselves, What am I doing that is correct? What am I doing that needs improvement? What in this lesson is working well? Why is this lesson not working? By developing a collaborative environment, they will learn to share credit from success. I never wanted to tell any teachers that they did badly while teaching the lesson, knowing that they put a good deal of time into thinking about the lesson and then teaching it. But, rather ask them "how do you improve this lesson?"

Students need to learn that graduation is not the final goal. More correctly, it should be called commencement, because commencement is the beginning of a whole new race.

Children need time to decompress and reflect, and school districts need to provide that time. Teachers also need time to recharge after constant exposure to the classroom environment. Research indicates that many teachers leave the profession because of physical and mental exhaustion. As author and former teacher Jessica Honard explained to Michael Godsey of the *Atlantic*, "It's a constant bombardment of social stimulation, and most teachers simply are not taught how to cope with it." Godsey wrote that the problem "for teachers in many cases is that they don't get any down time; they finish various meetings with various adults and go straight to the classroom, where they feel increasing pressure to facilitate social learning activities and promote the current trend of collaborative education." Former middle school teacher John Spencer told Godsey that teachers are "tired of being 'on' all the time . . . [and] they simply need time to recharge."

Effort does not guarantee positive outcomes. Grade achievement should not be based solely on participation or effort. A number of educators believe that every child who participates in a contest should be rewarded. While there are exceptions—Special Olympics being one— awards should be given for achievement. To do otherwise diminishes the achievement of the winners. Recognition should be given to those who participated, to encourage others—but not by awarding trophies. Likewise, a parent who says that "my child studies for several hours" but failed to pass the examination should be thanked for the effort—but the child should not be passed, because the effort failed to produce the desired results.

Teachers do what they are comfortable doing. Most teachers teach the way they were taught. If most, or many, of their own teachers were strict disciplinarians, in all probability they will be as well. The way we were taught, however, is not necessarily the way we should teach students.

Students process information differently. Some people need time to think and reflect, while others can come up with answers quickly. Teachers need to pause when asking a class questions, to accommodate the different learning styles of students.

There exist many barriers to student learning:

- Health challenges—in addition to colds, there are a large number of "childhood diseases," including chicken pox, mumps, and now a growing number of cases of measles.
- Their parents' own education and their support—parents need to prioritize education.
- Teachers need more time to learn how to teach.
- A traditional static classroom—teachers need to transform it into an interactive one.
- "Don't ever forget where you came from, but don't let it define you."
- "What did you do in the past three years that did not go well? How did you do about it?"

The Rumor Mill. All schools have a rumor mill. And some people love to feed the mill, creating "stories" that they might know are not true. It is difficult for most teachers, especially newly hired ones, to discern which ones are true. Administrators and/or fellow teachers need to squelch rumors as soon as they are aware of the rumors' existence. In order to retain people, you need to be honest and describe both the positives and negatives of the job of teaching. Many people are dulled by colleagues who have seen the negatives and have been burned out by the daily wearing down of their actions by students, parents, colleagues, and the system. They get lulled into the cadence that everybody else is in. Instead, they need to maintain the excitement they had when they first entered the job.

Educators Need to Identify Children's Strengths. Most educators can identify the weaknesses of their at-risk learners. All of us have weaknesses. Many children today face conditions that were practically unheard of not too many years ago—divorce, drugs, violent death, physical and mental abuse. I would have difficulty dealing with these situations, yet most of them do. Can educators identify the strengths of these learners—their ability to survive under dire circumstances, their desire to learn?

Lesson Planning

Baseball manager Billy Martin: *Preparation always shows itself in the spontaneity of the moment.* Proper planning prevents poor performance. Teachers need to be fully prepared to teach relevant, interesting lessons that meet the needs of all students and are aligned to the standards in every core subject taught. They need to squelch the idea of "shooting from the hip." When creating lesson plans, teachers need to determine what are the three things they want a lesson to achieve. At the end of the lesson, they can ask students, "What are the three most important things that you learned today?"

Legendary golfer Ben Hogan: *Golf is a matter of luck. The more you practice, the better your luck.* Teachers need to be given time to learn how to teach in front of real students. It takes time. It is one of the reasons for a three-to-five-year period before tenure is granted. Encourage new staff to learn, to practice, to share with colleagues. New teachers need to find a pathfinder to take them through the brambles and weeds: someone who has gone through the hurdles, knows where they are, and helps new teachers to avoid them. Ask for (rather than require) people to become mentors.

Qualities New Teachers and
New Administrators Should Possess

What are the qualities new teachers and new administrators should possess? Some of these are the following:

- a passion for learning,

- patience,

- politeness,

- integrity,

- honesty,

- transparency,

- common sense,

- dedication,

- selflessness,

- fairness,

- preparation to work hard for very long hours,

- flexibility,

- responsiveness to ranges of student abilities, and

- willingness to break down complex ideas into manageable chunks.

Questioning. Teachers need to be taught how to ask questions. How to elicit responses. How to really actively listen to students' responses. How to be comfortable with silence, because students need to digest, to assimilate, so they need time to respond. Teachers need to be flexible enough to deal with the responses they are given, which may not fit into their existing plans. Ask teachers: "What do you need to do your job? What do you need in order to be successful?"

Student Passivity. Teachers frequently reward passivity in students. If a student does not know the correct answer in a short period of time or does not even answer at all, the teacher moves on to another student. Teachers need to allow students to think and digest information before testing them on it.

Suspending Students. When looking at referrals for students who could or should be suspended, it is important to look at the reasons given. Many referrals request that a student be suspended or expelled because they were "disrespectful." It is equally important to identify who is submitting the referrals. Is it a new teacher who is having difficulty with classroom management? Are multiple referrals coming from the same individuals, and therefore it may be an adult problem as opposed to a child problem?

Family Engagement. Encourage parents to come to parent-teacher nights or parent-teacher conferences, especially to introduce new staff to parents. Supply tea or coffee and cookies. These meetings should be used to explain course and teacher expectations, explain attendance and grading policies, distribute important documents, and share contact information between the school and teachers and the parents. Have the new teachers speak and answer questions.

Technology. Computers can be a great ally in enhancing learning. Technology has the capacity of improving learning for all students. It adds a new dimension of learning through interactivity and its ability to correct errors without the criticism that may be expressed consciously or unconsciously by a teacher. For a potential dropout, who for a variety of reasons has difficulty interacting with humans or in a school setting, this added dimension can serve as a real boon to learning. But some technology can also distract students from doing schoolwork. Educators need to know that taking away a cell phone from a student is like taking away a limb.

Time. Education needs time to penetrate. Students need to take time to absorb as well as analyze. Learning needs to be designed so as to not only transmit information but also provide the ability to transform that information into knowledge. Is teaching 90 percent knowledge and 10 percent personality, or is it 90 percent personality and 10 percent knowledge? How many of us have ever had a teacher who knew the material but could not teach it? Think of your favorite teacher and determine what factors that individual had that "turned you on to want to learn."

Motivation. Children do not need to be motivated. They naturally are. However, after about five years they can become demotivated. The same is true for teachers. We need to identify what has demotivated them and remove those factors. Teach children how to think, not what to think. Industry wants students who not only know the material but also work in teams, are flexible, and can problem solve. Testing fixes the blame, not the process. We know that children who are in poverty, are minorities, or are special education students will, in general, not do as well on examinations as students who are more affluent and are white. If we wish to fix the process, we need to identify the root causes of the problem and attempt to address them. What causes children to do poorly in school, including on tests?

Agree on Classroom Rules at the Beginning of the Year

New teachers should be encouraged to develop a set of classroom rules at the beginning of the school term. The rules should be fair. Taking time for this simple step can prevent a lot of misery in the long term. Experienced educators suggest engaging students actively in the process of determining a set of class rules. Taking this preventive measure creates a positive climate from the start. This does not have to take long; even three minutes can make a difference. You can do this by asking questions such as, "What do you want to get out of class?" Teachers can weigh in with their goals for class too. This is a chance for the teacher, while still maintaining control of a classroom, to share with students at their level. It is a way to communicate with them. Making them feel like a part of the process sets a positive tone.

New staff needs to be consistent about expectations. When you are in a classroom with a teacher who reinforces positive behavior, kids calm down. If students or their work needs to be corrected, it needs to be done in a positive way. It should not be "You did it the wrong way," but rather help them see the right way to get the right results. Students need to be able to trust people, and they should believe that teachers are there to help, not to criticize. Staff needs to be consistent in their expectations and methods. Allow students to maintain their dignity. Do not make a big deal of a particular issue, in front of the whole class. Handle the situation quietly and calmly. Preventing classroom disruptions is more effective than dealing with these disruptions after they have taken place. Do not punish the class for the disruptions of an individual.

As quickly as possible, new teachers should learn the names of their students. No one likes to be anonymous in a group.

Greet your students at the door and nurture the relationships by taking an interest in their lives. Show students that you care! It has been said that if your students like you, then there is almost nothing that they will not do for you. Conversely, if your students do not like you, then there is almost nothing that they will not do *to* you!

Unlike other businesses, educators frequently have to "sell" something to people who do not want to buy it, whether they are students or parents. Educators do not have a lot of control over circumstances. Just when they think they do, conditions and circumstances change. Good educators are flexible, and they need to be. Not everything that they do works. They make rapid decisions on the spot and follow their gut. They must be adaptable to a variety of changing conditions. We have a wide and diverse learning group, all of whom we need to educate. We need to accept those children who do not learn in the same way that we teach. We need to teach them the way they are able to learn. We need to accommodate those students who, for whatever reason, color outside the lines.

CHAPTER 3

Leadership: The Backbone of School Improvement

"Accountability and higher standards have changed just about every aspect of education. [We need schools that] have dedicated teachers led by an instructional leader who has student achievement as the main goal of the school."

> — **Dr. Gene Bottoms**, vice president, Southern Regional Education Board

"Leadership is second only to classroom instruction among all school-related factors that contribute to what students learn at school."

> — **Wallace Foundation**, *How Leadership Influences Student Learning*

Learning How to Become a School Leader

According to research, there are more than fifteen thousand books on leadership in print. Articles on leadership increase in number by the thousands each year. The obvious conclusions that can be drawn from these facts are that there are more books and articles on leadership available than we can ever hope to read and that leadership clearly is a crucial and abiding topic of interest to countless women and men in society. Despite the popularity of the topic, however, educational leadership remains a paradox. People who seek to understand it by reading a primer on the topic will inevitably be frustrated and disappointed. Leaders transcend the confines of a defining box. First of all, leaders are not born but evolve into that role. According to Warren Bennis, a noted authority on leadership quoted in a blog by Michael Shinagel, "The most dangerous leadership myth is that leaders are born—that there is a genetic factor to leadership. That's nonsense; in fact, the opposite is true. Leaders are made rather than born." Obviously, schools of education believe this because they spend much time attempting to teach leadership to large numbers of people. But universities do not prepare you for the real world of education. People can describe to you what it means to be a school leader, but you do not really know until you become one. Leadership needs to be experienced. People look to you for guidance, wanting your time and anticipating your "expertise." But reading about leadership will not necessarily result in excellent leadership. My mentor, the MIT organizational theorist Dr. Myron Tribus, taught that one could read all the books about swimming and take tests to demonstrate your knowledge, but you cannot become a swimmer until you learn by getting into the pool. Reading leadership books, while helpful, can do only so much to teach about leadership. In addition to reading as many books and blog posts as you can, it is important to attend conferences, speak to others, and find out how they handle real-life problems.

Listen, Discuss, Read. As a school leader, you will have many demands on your time. Nevertheless, you should encourage others to observe you, and be receptive to their criticism and advice to improve your own practice. One way to do this is to volunteer to teach a class, and invite teachers who have free time to come and observe you. Ask them to attend a debriefing afterward, discuss what they observed, and make suggestions for you to improve. When you use an idea you have gathered from someone else, make sure the rest of the staff know where the credit is due.

In addition, keep up-to-date on current thinking in the world of education. For example, read one current book about education during each of the longer school holidays, and then discuss with others what you read, thought about, and learned. Start a staff educational library, if one does not already exist. Include teaching videos from YouTube and TED talks. Reading blogs is also an excellent way of keeping up to speed, and writing blogs—for example, about your leadership journey—will help you to reflect and learn. Use Twitter for educational development, and encourage others to do the same. My first principal, Irving Anker, scheduled all new teachers to have the same lunch period so they could discuss their common problems. Every Friday, we had lunch in his office, where he would discuss with us a book or article he had read. I still fondly remember those lunches.

Continue to grow as a professional. Develop your self-awareness by actively seeking and acting on constructive criticism from others whose professional judgment you trust. Which skills or areas of professional knowledge do you need to strengthen? How can you go about this? Show you are aware that, however experienced you are, you will never finish learning. Make yourself dispensable. What greater legacy can you leave than that the organization is running well without you? It means that you have selected the right people who can do great things even without you. As Lao Tzu put it, "A leader is best when people barely know he exists, when his work is done, his aim fulfilled, they will say: we did it ourselves."

Leaders learn to become leaders, and they continue to learn in their role as leaders. I have worked for some of the best principals and for some who were not so good. I learned from both. I learned things I should do and what not to do. I will never forget my first day on the job: it was a cold, ugly day in New York, with the added bonus of a teachers' strike. It was also the first day for Irving Anker, the new principal. He had the dietitian supply coffee and tea for people walking the picket line. By the time the strike ended, his actions had changed the way people saw him. People watch school leaders to see how they dress, how they speak to people, the example they set. You need to form your own view of leadership.

When I first became a supervisor, one of the first things I did was to buy a large coffeepot and bring it into my office. It encouraged people to visit the office and became a place for staff members to get together.

The Job of School Leader

New Responsibilities Require New Qualifications. In olden days, we could sum up the principal's role in a few words: to manage the building and head the school; to be a *pal* to students, parents, and teachers; to be a leader of teachers. But that role has dramatically expanded.

Consider the leadership responsibilities outlined for today's principals: the job of a school leader has become increasingly complex, adding new responsibilities and obligations. School administrators have been tasked with improving instruction, safety concerns, and evaluations of staff. In all, they have to deal with

- the U.S. Department of Education,
- the state Department of Education,
- the local school board,
- school security issues,
- teachers,
- students,
- parents,
- special education students and their families,
- unions,
- bus drivers,
- custodians,
- cafeteria workers,
- recruiting new staff,
- retaining staff,
- refreshing existing staff.

All this has to be achieved while attempting to balance work and personal life.

Most of an educational leader's time is spent managing the school. This requires that the principal have the skills and competencies appropriate for businesses as well as the schoolhouse. But, contrary to popular opinion, the principal is not the CEO of the school. At best, the principal is the middle manager in a system of rules, regulations, and mandates from above—at the bottom of the pyramid of true policy makers.

Likewise, we expect much more of today's school superintendents. We no longer select them simply because of what they know about education, child development, teaching, or learning. They come to us from the ranks of business, the military, political power structures, or the legal profession. Frequently, they are managers, not educators.

But command-and-control theory no longer works in education—not in the classroom or in the administration of schools. The days when principals and/or superintendents could simply order people to do things are over. Traditional top-down models of school leadership do not work in an educational environment where workers possess as much education and experiential knowledge as the nominal leader. Only collaboration will get the job done. There needs to be a shift to shared leadership with classroom teachers taking greater responsibility at the school level, not just in their own classrooms.

What follows are some of the responsibilities related to educational leadership:

The Principal as a Leader

- Facilitate and implement a comprehensively developed and shared vision and mission.

- Implementation must include the development of structures to support the vision and mission.

- Create a culture of high expectations for all students.

- Expectations must be communicated to staff, students, parents, and the wider community, and actions must consistently reflect those expectations.

- Model ethical conduct and universally expect the same from faculty and staff.

- Expectations must be clearly explained and consistently enforced.

- Empower others to make significant decisions.

- Expanding the foundation of leadership stabilizes any organization.

- Nurture teacher involvement and engender teacher leadership.

- Teacher leaders take ownership of the school and its processes.

- Comprehensive input and involvement in the decision-making processes improve the chances of making the best available decision.

The Principal as a Lead Teacher and Learner

- Sustain a school culture conducive to student and staff learning.

- Ensure the use of research-based strategies that support a cooperatively developed curriculum.

- Promote the use of research-based programs as a means of achieving the school's objectives.

- Participate in focused and sustained professional development that implements, nurtures, and sustains research-based learning and teaching.

- Provide focused and comprehensive instructional leadership.

- Model effective learning strategies while participating in professional development with staff.

The Principal as the Face of the School

- Attend community events.

- Promote the school.

- Increase school involvement in the community.

- Ensure that steps are taken that guarantee improved educational experience for each student.

- Improve the plight of students, which improves the perception of their parents.

- Put structures in place that promote individualized instruction (mentoring, learning centers, remediation, etc.).

- Work to develop cooperative relationships between the school and the surrounding community.

- Use the resources of the community.

- Allow the community to use the school's resources.

The Principal as a Manager

- Develop and manage the school budget.

- Ensure that budget decisions reflect a commitment to the school's mission and vision.

- Select and evaluate instructional staff.

- Make staff decisions based on student and learning needs.

- Evaluate teachers based on their ability to successfully fulfill the tenets of the school's mission and vision.

- Deal with discipline and attendance concerns.

- Provide a safe and orderly learning environment.

- Maintain accountability for an effective and aligned instructional program.

- Ensure compliance with state and federal mandates.

And the job remains daunting. We judge our principals and superintendents by a new bottom line: their students' academic success. In the 1960s, 1970s, and 1980s, we cared about equality of access and opportunity. Today, with the emphasis on higher standards, we focus on proficiency of achievement. We no longer expect school leaders to simply usher students through the grades at a level of learning that matches the population or its special needs. Each year, the numbers must show improvement. Politicians, business leaders, the media, the general public, and the parents of students expect excellence in every school district, school, and classroom.

School Leaders Are Made, Not Born

Scratch the surface of an excellent school and you will find an excellent leader. Conversely, consider a failing school and you will find weak leadership. According to research described in a report by Kenneth Leithwood and Carolyn Riehl, leadership has a significant effect on student learning, second only to the effects of the quality of curriculum and teachers' instruction.

Few professions train their leaders. We can think of two: business and the military. In the past, education has looked to these as models. Granted, certain leadership qualities transcend those fields, and a few innovative businesses have redefined the corporate culture to draw on the skills and abilities of their workforce. In general, however, both business and the military use a *cascade* model, in which leadership flows from the well-trained, knowledgeable, and educated cadre at the top to the less trained or educated workers at the bottom. As we have noted, education is not like that; classroom teachers are knowledgeable, well-educated professionals. Their leaders need a specific set of skills.

Often, we select our principals from the ranks of good teachers, good classroom managers, or superior teacher mentors. Too often, we fail to consider the skills, attitudes, and characteristics essential to effective leadership—and especially instructional leadership. Likewise, many college and university programs that train educational leaders work with individuals who choose administrative programs. Not many leadership programs go into the field to identify potential educational leaders. There is a huge difference between managing a school and leading instruction. Few principals do both well.

And yet, we believe that America's schools can improve. We believe that with effective training, greater resources, and support through mentoring, principals and superintendents can lead the way. Across America, we find examples of excellence—leaders who firmly believe

46

that *all* children can succeed, schools that effectively meet the needs of nontraditional learners, and educational communities that do not give up on their at-risk students.

Developing Business Partnerships

School budgets have been shrinking as demands for services and costs have increased. Many schools are involved with the business community, yet few have developed plans to help their business partners know what they need and want. What follows is a business partnership plan that I developed for my school:

Dear business partner,

We would like you to consider helping us in the following ways:

- **Curriculum**
  Reviewing, revising, and developing curriculum so that graduating students will be trained to current standards.

- **Equipment**
  New, used, or broken, but repairable and able to fit existing programs.

- **Jobs for Students**
  Co-op, after school, summer, and after graduation.

- **Paid Externships**
  For teachers to upgrade skills and create awareness in students of what skills and qualities are need in the business world.

- **Business Training Workshops**

  Workshops for teachers and students to learn techniques necessary for teaching employment skills (i.e., management, résumé writing, computer programs).

- **Funds**

  Contributions to maintain and further develop existing programs and to provide college scholarships for graduating students.

- **Businesspeople on Loan**

  Your people with expertise to speak to classes, to provide mock interviews, and to help with résumé preparation.

Teamwork and Consensus. Form a leadership team. Everyone in it needs to be reading from the same book and to be on the same page—if they are not, there will be a chasm within the organization. The team needs to speak with a single voice. Hold meetings and come to an agreement through consensus and compromise, followed by the need for everyone to support the decision. Of course, there can be differences of opinion. Waiting to make the perfect decision may mean that you do not make any decision. But once a strategy has been decided, everyone needs to stand behind it. That is critical. You cannot always achieve consensus, but you need to be able to stand back and say, "That's good enough."

At the same time, choose people who think differently from you. They give you diverse points of view and a diversity of thought. Good leaders will find a way to have these diverse ideas work together. Hire not only highly qualified but highly effective staff. Have you ever had a teacher who knew all the material but could not teach? We all have. School leaders need to identify not only highly qualified teachers but also highly effective teachers.

Widening the Circle

Principals need to realize that they not supposed to have all the answers. Their job is to surround themselves with people who can help figure out the answers.

Strategic Planning

School leaders need to be proactive, but educators tend to be risk-averse. They become comfortable with the status quo, even if it is not working as well as it should. How do you motivate the educational team to take risks? Educational leaders need to make things happen. They cannot expect others to do it in their place. I was an assistant soccer coach for my son's team. Before every game, the coach told the players to "make it happen. Nobody will give you anything unless you make it happen. The other team wants to win as much as you do. If you want to win, you need to make it happen." This is good advice not just for sports but also for life. Organize teams among teachers and students, because then they support one another. Everyone is valuable on a team because they offer different perspectives and have different skills and strengths. Are you aware of the strengths and weakness of your team members?

They need to anticipate things and not only make strategic plans but also arrange to deploy those strategies by assigning jobs, providing timetables, and offering adequate resources (both time and money). If you have not developed a strategy, you are going to fail. In education, we spend a great deal of time developing strategic plans and an insufficient time on strategic deployment. We rarely study the results of the implementation process and fail to develop new strategic plans. I have been in schools where it felt as if we were doing something for the first time and continued to make the same mistakes that we had made the previous time.

Problem Solving

As smart and talented as educators are, they are still looking for a leader to point them in the right direction and help them take the next step. Leaders are expected to solve problems. How do leaders spend their time? Time is the most precious resource for a school principal. Waiting for a perfect time to solve problems or waiting for the perfect solution to a problem may result in never solving the problem. Real leadership is achieved by giving somebody the capacity to solve his or her own problems by exploring the possibilities. Ask them great questions and lead them to possible alternatives. If you say, "Here is the problem and here is your solution," you are just building resistance. It is OK not to have all of the answers and not to be able to do everything. As a leader, you need to say, "I need your help." People want to help; they just need to be asked.

Dr. Russell Ackoff was a brilliant organizational theorist and professor emeritus of management science at the Wharton School, University of Pennsylvania. As he described in his book *The Art of Problem Solving*, Dr. Ackoff developed the following "Four Ways of Problem Solving"

1. Absolve: "It's not my problem; I can ignore it."

2. Resolve the problem: The disadvantage of this method is that because the causes have not been dealt with, the problem will reappear.

3. "Solve the problem" By selecting this method, you remove the causes and the problem should not reappear. Most people favor this technique.

4. The best solution is to "dissolve the problem"—prevent it before it appears. Predict what problems will arise and work to prevent their occurrence.

How are problems addressed in your school? Does the school absolve itself of any responsibility? Or does the school attempt to dissolve the problem? Problems are going to happen, and it is a supervisor's job to help teachers and counselors with their problems. Most problems cannot be solved by one person alone. Ask yourself what help *you* need and who can provide it. Be willing to take risks. It is acceptable to be uncertain about the unknown. But not taking risks means that you are willing to accept the status quo. Encourage staff never to present a problem without also presenting possible solutions. Education has many problems, and some staff people like to point them out. If you get bogged down in all the problems that are out there—and there will always be problems—then you will never be able to move forward. Acknowledge the problems but emphasize the positive. While a leader needs to make decisions, do not waffle around. If you do, the people you lead will become frustrated and not know what to do. You will make mistakes, but you are better off than if you did nothing. Hold yourself back; get the opinions of others. Let the organization solve the problem. I have asked, "If you were me, how would you deal with this problem?" People want to have their opinions expressed but also want to help solve problems. Give employees a role in solving problems.

One solution does not solve all problems. It is very situational. Instead of merely bringing problems, people need to bring a solution. Ask people, "How would you solve this problem?" Work on complex problems by breaking them down into smaller pieces and figuring out a path to take. Admit your mistakes. Nobody is perfect. Figure out what part of the problem you are responsible for. And learn from your mistakes. If people bring you problems to solve, ask them, "If I weren't here, how would you solve the problem?" More often than not, their instinct is correct because they are dealing with the problem on a day-to-day basis. Do not look for just the "lowest hanging fruit." Certain problems are easier to address. But not addressing the more difficult problems simply allows them to infect the fundamental roots of the organization, ultimately poisoning it. Tell your staff that you want to avoid surprises. Ask, "What do you think I should know?" You cannot fix a problem if you do not know it exists. Hire good people and give them the opportunity to do what they need to do. If something is going to happen, it is easier to prepare for it as opposed to reacting to it. You do not want to be surrounded by people who will not tell you the truth.

Risk-Taking

Leaders need to take calculated risks based on their own personal experiences and training, as well as others'. Other people are going through the same difficulties as you, so why not tap into their strategies, experience, and expertise? If you have a problem, ask a colleague how he or she handled it. Identify what obstacles prevent you from delivering a favorable result. That means taking responsibility when something is not producing the best results. Hire people who have skills you do not have, who are smarter than you are. You do not have to know everything. Do not hire only people who agree with you. You need to get as much input as possible to know what is happening. Jill Berry is an educational consultant. She wrote a chapter in *Don't Change the Light Bulbs: A Compendium of Expertise from the UK's Most Switched-On Educators*, edited by Rachel Jones, including this: "You won't have the same responsibilities as classroom teachers with full teaching timetables, but don't forget what it feels like to be in their shoes. It's important to help them to do the best job they can, rather than making it tougher. If you receive feedback from any source that you are adding to staff stress rather than supporting them with the demanding elements of their role, then you need to do some hard thinking about how you can redress this. The most important thing in any school is the quality of the pupils' experience."

Ed Bales, a friend, mentor, and retired vice president at Motorola, gave me the following leadership examples, describing five groups of individuals in every organization:

- First come the Scouts. These individuals are receptive to all changes, recognizing that what already exists is not working as well as it could. Because they are so visible, they are subject to being targeted.

- They are followed by the Pioneers. These individuals are also receptive to change, but they are less likely to make the first move.

- The pioneers are followed by the Settlers. The Settlers are willing to accept change as well but are not willing to be highly visible.

- In back of the settlers come the Resisters. The resisters dislike change and will resist changing the culture.

- They are followed by the Saboteurs. Saboteurs are exactly as their name implies. They not only resist but will do everything in their power to stop and overthrow every proposed change. They have a vested interest in maintaining the status quo.

Can you name the people in your school or district who are representative of each group? Which group is the most valuable to you as a school leader? Which group is the most dangerous? Which group should be drawn closest? Which group should you maintain a distance from?

Tell People the Truth

This involves being honest. It has to be done positively, sensitively, constructively, and professionally, but it has to be done. Do not lie to teachers. When you observe a bad lesson, tell the teacher, while giving suggestions to make it better. Ask the teacher to arrange to observe an admired colleague and get suggestions from that person. Ask the teacher if he or she would mind being mentored. Show empathy—but be honest. It is hard to deliver bad news, and part of leadership is giving people permission to give you bad news. You simply cannot ask, "What did you think of the lesson?" Because the answer you get may be the one you do not want to hear. Lawyers have the right idea: do not ask a question that you do not know the answer to.

Educators need to be flexible. Anything can happen in a classroom at any time. Leaders make sure the pieces fit together smoothly and appear effortless. But in schools, people work as individuals (students studying for a test; teachers developing lesson plans and curricula). Leaders need to encourage people to work together on teams in order to collaborate. Individuals need to work together not in competition but for the betterment of students, parents, and the school.

If you ask for advice, follow it—or explain why not. It is not about giving up control. It is not about consensus. School leadership needs to be transparent. Make sure you are involving others along the way. You always need to improve what you are doing, even though you have good things going. And do not promise what you cannot deliver. I once had a principal who gave me the following advice: "Start by saying no." This technique often discouraged people from advancing any new ideas to the principal. His belief was that if you were started with no, you would be a hero if people could convince you with their arguments to switch to yes. People need to trust you and you need to trust them. It is easy to say that you trust people, but that must be demonstrated.

Admit you may be wrong, that you may have to come up with better ways of doing things. This means not believing that you always know best but instead are able to assimilate ideas from other people and take the best ideas. Administrators need to be transparent and straight, telling it like it is.

Parents

Parents are more concerned with school safety than anything else. They want to send their child to school and be assured that their child is learning in a safe environment. Provide the safest environment for all youngsters. At school, they should be safer than in their homes and the streets they walk on in their neighborhoods.

Administrators need to provide in their school budgets for these additional costs; they need to organize parental car pools and to work with law enforcement officials. Schools need to be friendly as well as safe. People—children, parents, teachers, and all other staff) need to want to go there and spend as much time as necessary in the school. And people need leaders to follow. But the best leaders lead in part by letting others manage things. A leader is very clear on the direction he or she wants to move and, with the involvement of staff, provides the direction, the vision (by empowering others), and the speed that the organization needs to proceed. A manager needs to monitor what is happening to ensure that there are no "hiccups" in the operation of a school. Both are important, and they need to function in tandem. A good leader is less concerned with the methods and means by which something is done and more concerned with the results.

Set Up a Vision

You need to present your vision so that others understand it. It is one of the reasons why actors rehearse. It is not a bad idea for educational leaders to rehearse what they are going to say to a group of people.

Team Building

Leaders cannot do it alone. The job is too overwhelming. For maximum effectiveness, there needs to be a leadership team, not just a leadership person. Leaders need to ensure that their vision and mission is deployed. How do they motivate the team to help carry out the leader's vision and goals? This is done by both words and actions. Leaders need to cut a path for others to follow. Building consensus is extremely hard. Trust is a key word in building teams. Trust must be authentic. But it takes time to build trust. The easiest way to build trust is to be consistent. The staff needs to develop a mutual vision of where the school needs to go. That vision is shared through a mission statement. Mission statements should be developed by the faculty, not only by the principal. Have a team develop a mission statement, then present it to the entire faculty to get them to "buy in." The downside of doing this is that it can take a long time. The upside is broader acceptance. Revisit it on a regular basis to see if it needs to be changed. The mission statements that I frequently see are so generic that they lack meaning or so specific that they are unachievable: "We are going to be the best high school, graduating the best students and achieving a 100 percent graduation rate." Mission statements should be SMART—specific, measurable, achievable over time, realistic, and time framed.

Visibility. Be visible and approachable. I remember when I was teaching a class and the principal came in to observe. After the principal left, a student asked, "Who was that guy?" Try to get out of your office as much as possible. Be a positive presence around the school, building relationships with staff, parents, and pupils. Principals should not spend breaks and lunchtimes catching up with e-mails. Attend extracurricular activities. Students and staff will become aware your presence indicates that they are going above and beyond their normal school day and that you value their contributions. Make sure that the pupils know you are interested in their experiences and achievements beyond the classroom, and that the staff running such activities see that you value their contribution. Leaders should be willing to "jump into the trenches." They need to offer to teach classes and invite teachers in to make suggestions for improvement. Never ask staff members to do anything you would not be willing to do yourself, even if that means" getting your hands dirty" to get the job done. Keep in mind, however, that there is a thin line between actively solving problems and instead allowing staff to find solutions to their problems. Try to coach people rather than jumping in and doing the work for them. Instead of giving people advice, leaders have the desire to do it for them. People need to feel they are part of the process rather than being an observer to it. Leaders need to know that they cannot do everything, nor can they do everything well. Create a leadership council composed of people who wish to be future leaders. Leaders build leaders. Constantly be in search of leaders from within the school and develop those interested in becoming leaders. Measure results, not efforts. People like to say that they are working hard—and they may be. But are they producing demonstrable results?

Great principals are in their schools early in the morning and stay late at night. As one teacher explained it, "He squeezes twenty-eight hours into twenty-four." They can be seen at sporting events and band concerts, and they pick up trash and plant flowers on the campus. They spend their days working with teachers on instruction, dealing with student discipline, and communicating with parents and others in the community. During their "off" time, they are reading educational research materials in an effort to find strategies that will enable their teachers to make a difference in their classrooms. There is a palpable spirit in a school that has a good leader. It can be felt when listening to students and is seen on the hallway walls. Everything is a celebration, and everyone in the school is happy to be there. Academic success is cheered just as athletics are, and teachers and students know they are valued. Visitors who come in the building will think, "This would be a great place to work!" You can measure the school leader's success when staff runs into the building on Monday morning as quickly as they run out on Friday afternoon. Even though there is a sense of urgency concerning learning and student achievement, everyone from the cafeteria staff and the custodians to the students, teachers, and office staff will announce with pride that they have the best school and would not want to be anywhere else.

Great principals work diligently to ensure that their teachers are equipped to be leaders in the classroom. Resources and supplies are available, and opportunities for professional development are strongly encouraged. Student leadership is also valued in schools with great principals. Students are given opportunities to excel in areas of interest to them, whether they are athletes or members of the chess club. And principals serve as important mentors to their assistant principals and interns.

Great principals make an effort to include families in the community of a school. They offer various opportunities for parents, including parent advisory councils, open house nights, question-and-answer sessions, and frequent communication via phone messages, e-mails, and publications sent home with the students.

Meetings

I view meetings in education as a "necessary evil." It makes it easy to deliver, to a large group of people, a message or series of messages quickly. Yet, according to an article by Drake Baer in *Business Insider*, $37 billion is lost every year as a result of mistakes at unproductive meetings. Writing in the *New York Times Magazine*, Virginia Heffernan stated that 15 percent of an organization's time is spent at meetings. What are the pros and cons of meetings? Some people consider meetings thieves of joy, of productivity, of mental freedom. But others bring new ideas that thrive at meetings. In the end, meetings are an important way for the leadership team come to agreements that everyone can stand behind.

How long should a meeting last? Have you ever gone to an excruciating meeting? A meeting where you wanted to walk out? After an hour, meetings reach a point of diminishing returns. You can tell that a meeting is becoming ineffective when people start fidgeting, looking at their watches, playing games on their smartphones, sending texts, reading e-mails, trying to stay awake—or sleeping. Prior to the meeting, know exactly what you hope to achieve. We have all attended meetings that lacked a purpose. They were held because somewhere it was written that a meeting had to take place. Meetings should not be held merely because they are on the calendar and are held every month; they should be held only if there is a purpose. Have an itemized list of what needs to get decided. Have the agenda distributed in advance so people will know what is to be discussed. Include action items, where people volunteer or are assigned a task. The chair position should be rotated so that everyone gets a turn to be "leader." We have all attended meetings where somebody filibusters or wants to show off. The person in charge needs to move the agenda, diplomatically. In addition, appoint a secretary to write a one- or two-page summary of what has taken place at the meeting. How large should a meeting be? I prefer small ones, of four to six people, because that is where actions get taken. Small meetings focus on problem solving as opposed to just giving and receiving information. Large meetings cause people to lose focus. See how many iPods and tablets come out as people become unfocused. As a result, they can do more harm than good.

Keys to successful meetings:

- Schedule shorter meetings; if necessary, hold a second meeting.

- Send materials in advance.

- Start and end on time. According to research, 37 percent of meetings start late because someone shows up late.

- Avoid monologues.

- Do not use buzzwords or clichés: People will recognize that they have heard these expressions before and will ignore them.

- Stay focused.

- Do not use phones during meetings. Do not even put them on tables. Put them in a pocket or a purse, and keep them on vibrate—if you must—and leave the room if you have to take a call. Using phones or tablets during meeting is rude and distracting. E-mails, texts, and tweets can wait.

- Capture key points and action items. And then distribute them. End the meeting with an action plan. Who will do what? When? What resources (time, money) are needed?

- The worst thing is to be at a meeting and be able to tell that people do not want to be there. Look for glazed eyes or other signs of boredom—crossed arms, doodling, sleeping.

- Establish ground rules. Criticize ideas, not people, respect different points of view, and do not have people try to "sell" their perspective to others.

- Listen to the expert rather than the loudest people in the room. Just because they are loud does not mean they are right.

- Have a facilitator, who contributes structure and brings the discussion back to the topic when people go off on tangents. He or she also acts as a timekeeper.

- Answer the following questions beforehand:

   1. Is the meeting necessary? Many meetings are held only because they are on the calendar.

   2. Who should attend? Make a list of required versus optional attendees.

People want to make a difference. They need to be provided with an opportunity to do well and positively affect the learning of children. Most people learn from the mistakes they make and attempt to improve.

The Most Important Person in the School

Who is the most important person in a school? It is not the highest paid or the person with a name on the door. It is the person the public sees or hears. It may be the secretary who answers the phone or the person sitting at the front door. They are the ones who have to face people who may be angry or hostile. They are the face of the school. If they do their job correctly, principals and deans may never see an angry or frustrated person. So make sure they are well trained. Acknowledge them! Reward them with flowers, letters, or simply words of thanks. Have you ever been frustrated by your phone call being answered by a machine or by a message such as, "Your call is important to us, but due to an unusually high volume of calls, the current wait time is thirty minutes"?

There are a variety of cliques in schools. There is a group of "newbies": people who have just joined the educational establishment and believe they can beat the system. Then there are the old-timers: those who have been around forever and believe they know the answers to all the problems in the school because they have seen everything.

What is the most important quality a leader needs to possess? When I have asked educators in my workshops, I get all sorts of answers: good personality, a vision, a sense of humor. For me, the most important quality is to have followers. A leader without followers is simply a person out for a walk. The job of educational leader is too complex and too overwhelming for a single person to do it on his or her own. An effective leader plants seed for others to water, take care, and make sure that things flourish. But the job of a high-quality leader is not to merely create followers but to create new leaders. Part of the job of leadership is to empower others to create "stretch goals." Schools leaders operate in a fishbowl. Everyone sees what you do. When you trip, everyone sees you fall. Create a leadership council composed of people who wish to be future leaders. Leaders build leaders. They are constantly in search of leaders from within their school and develop those interested in becoming a leader.

If a teacher or group consistently outperforms another, you need to ask why and how it was able to achieve that success, and how it can be replicated in the rest of the department or school. We need to ask, how did you learn to do what you do? Or what lessons have you learned that you are willing to share with others? Educators need to work together in teams. Establish study groups for teachers. The bulk of modern work is team based. Yet education is predominantly a single individual's work. Teacher lesson plans, tests, and curricula are generally done alone and are not frequently shared. Similarly, students in K–12 learning environments are encouraged to work and study alone. But studies show that groups tend to innovate faster. Groups see mistakes more quickly and find better solutions to problems. As a *New York Times Magazine* article by Charles Duhigg noted, studies show that people working in teams tend to achieve better results and report higher job satisfaction. The most successful teams work for successful leaders. There needs be direct, frank, and open communication. Seek the advice of all stakeholders and ask questions far more than making statements. Peter Senge, in his book *The Fifth Discipline*, stated that organizations in general need to be learning organizations. That applies to schools as well. Most schools see themselves as teaching organizations, but the reality is that they should be learning organizations. That applies to teachers, parents, students, and school leaders. Try to encourage learning in the school. Schools have become too complex to expect a single person to have all the answers all the time. With the possible exception of hospitals, no organization has a higher educational level than the people who work in schools. Imagine the multiplier effect of bringing their ideas and unique experiences together to solve problems.

Many businesses fail because they want the right things but measure the wrong things and therefore get the wrong results. Turning a school around is like turning around a large ship. It takes time and requires a strong leader. The primary job of school leaders is to improve instruction. But the typical principal only spends about 20 percent of his or her time on instruction. Schools need a second leader who handles managing the schools so that the principal can improve instruction.

Thoughts on Leadership

What follows is a variety of thoughts about elements of great leadership, and the impact a great leader—or a bad one—can have.

A key thing I have learned in my career and my own work experience: Bad managers tell employees what to do, good managers explain why they need to do it, but great managers involve people in decision making and improvement. Bad managers bark orders. They are directive and tell employees what to do, without any explanation or context. I saw a lot of that style of management quite often during my first two years in education, and the workplace was incredibly dysfunctional as a result. There are top-down, command-and-control managers in every type of workplace, unfortunately. Managers who are controlling and have all the answers want their employees to "check their brains at the door," and they often say so quite explicitly—or they spread that message in more subtle ways. Front-line employees (teachers, counselors, dietitians, bus drivers, custodians) complained that they were "hired for their backs and their arms, not their brains."

Bob Kattman: "A poor principal causes disharmony. A good principal minds the school. The best principal drives the school."

Do you have positional power as opposed to personal power? Do you have power because of the position you occupy or because of who you are? What gives you power is how you treat people and how you lead them.

Lead by example, not "Do what I say" or "Do what I want."

Give people some flexibility, within reason, to make decisions. Allow people to come up with an action plan.

You need to create consistency in students' experiences from class to class and grade to grade.

Although you want everyone to like you, you need to make tough decisions that some people will disagree with. You need to be more concerned with the success of the organization than with your own success as an individual.

If your school were going to be named the best school of the year in five years, what would it look like? What would you and your staff have done? What would you have accomplished? As an employee, what would you need from me? As a supervisor, what would I expect from you? What is the road that will get us there?

A leader needs to be at his or her best under pressure.

It is not how well you do as a leader, but how well you help others do their best, that matters most.

School administrators need to create an environment of transparency so that the rumor mill will not derail improvements.

You focus on the opportunities rather than the obstacles.

You hire people to do everything but hire people. So if it is somebody else's job, do not do it.

Make difficult calls quickly and confidently.

Schools need to determine, "What are you doing here? What do you want to stand for?"

It is difficult to develop plans and deploy them because schools are subject to so much change, so frequently.

Because parents are the first teachers of children—they teach their child how to speak, how to walk, how to use the bathroom—they need to be encouraged to become an active part of their child's learning.

Teachers can get discouraged if they look at how much farther they have to go as opposed to the distance they have traveled, so they need to have their courage constantly reinforced.

We need to question the ideas we inherit.

Always be honest, candid, and fair.

People do not spend enough time communicating, and lack of communication leads to lack of trust. If classroom teachers cannot trust their leaders, then they will question any and all decisions made. Try not to lie. How can people trust someone who gives you their word and then goes back on it? Leaders believe we can do things better and faster than the people in our charge, but we also need to let go and allow them to make mistakes. Be patient with staff and students. We frequently want things done as quickly as possible. I had a supervisor who said, "ASAY." I said that I understood she meant "ASAP—as soon as possible." No, she said, she wanted it as soon as yesterday.

Principals are held accountable for their actions.

What is more important: being a friend or being a supervisor?

Actions speak louder than words. Who is the best supervisor you had? What made him or her the best?

Any organization that is not moving forward when others are is, in reality, moving backward.

Squelch the idea of "shooting from the hip." Prepare.

Administrators need to teach classes. This allows them to know what people do every day. It shows teachers that you understand what they go through. The classes that an administrator teaches should not be the best class in the grade; it may be the lowest. Invite teachers to come, observe, and critique the lesson.

Choose your battles carefully, because you cannot win every battle.

You have to learn how to fail.

Courage is one word that should be in every educator's vocabulary. Taking risks can lead to failure—but it can also lead to success. The fear of failure inhibits educators from taking risks. By not taking risks, educators are basically supporting the status quo.

Vince Lombardi: It is not how often you get knocked down; it is how frequently you get up.

Give each person a second chance.

Create an environment where people can grow and thrive.

Everybody is replaceable, including you. Train others to become leaders.

A positive attitude is as important as knowledge. Knowledge is easily obtainable. Some people see only the limits to their success.

Bad bosses only leave scars on their employees. They criticize them in public, in front of their peers. They use hurtful, emotional words to bring them down. People long remember the hurt that is leveled by bosses.

Management expert Gary Hamel was once asked, "How will you know if you are a great leader?" He replied, "Turn around and see if anyone is following you."

Listen

Educators need to listen. You need to have the ability to take a step back, absorb what others are saying, and fuse it with your ideas. I never found out much by listening to myself. Steve Covey, the author of *The 7 Habits of Highly Effective People*: "Seek first to be understood, then to understand." First you have to listen to be understood. If you are like most people, you probably seek first to be understood; you want to get your point across. And in doing so, you may ignore the other person completely, pretend you are listening, selectively hear only certain parts of the conversation, or attentively focus only on the words being said, but miss the meaning entirely. So why does this happen? Because most people listen with the intent to reply, not to understand. You listen to yourself as you prepare in your mind what you are going to say, the questions you are going to ask, etc. You filter everything you hear through your own life experiences, your frame of reference. You check what you hear against your autobiography and see how it measures up. Consequently, you decide prematurely what the other person means before he or she finishes communicating. Does any of the following sound familiar? You can't have a preestablished agenda until you have listened to the agendas of your constituents. When you are listening to someone, you need to pay attention to, and process, what the other person is saying, not focus on formulating your response. Listening is the key to learning. And that means listening to all the people in the organization, not just those at the top of the pyramid. The people doing the work are those who are likeliest to have answers to the problems that arise. Ask staff to identify their major problems. Then respond, "Now tell me what you suggest to solve it." It is easy to identify problems; it is more difficult to try to solve them. One lesson is to try to be the best listener you know how to be.

In education, luck has nothing to do with success. Educators need to plan, and to have contingency plans. Teachers should be able to give a good reason for any decision they make. ("Why did you emphasize this in your lesson plan?") You want them to be able to defend their decisions. Teachers should be coachable. You give them feedback and want to see how they react to it. Either they are learning or they are arguing with you. Are they "yessing" you because they think that is what you want to hear?

I have dealt with almost every teacher, parent, and student issue imaginable, and I am still learning that there are things I do not know how to deal with. All educators need to take charge of the situation and get people excited about learning. Educators have to put a spotlight on learning.

Reaching a Goal

If you want to reach a goal, you must set up a target. A strategic plan gets you from the current state to a desired future state.

- Create a common understanding of how you got to where you are now.
- Take a quick look at your current situation.
- Envision the future.
- What would have to happen to create the desired future?
- Develop action plans.
- Deploy action plans.
- SWOT Analysis (Strengths, Weaknesses, Opportunities, Threats)

Goals are simply plateaus—once they have been reached, gather the energy to get to the next! We become complacent about the things we do well and become fearful of taking any risks because of the fear of failure. The borders that we set for ourselves, handicap us.

Exit-Out or Stay-In Interviews

Schools make major investments in the people they hire. They normally do not know the cost of those investments if they lose their best people, and as noted near the beginning of the Introduction, a report by the Alliance for Excellent Education puts a conservative estimate of the cost of replacing public school teachers who have dropped out of the profession at $2.2 billion a year. While there is a dollar value involved, the schools that lose the most teachers disproportionately serve students of color and students from low-income families. What is difficult, if not impossible, to measure is the disruption of learning caused by the departure of trained, experienced educators. It undermines student achievement and consumes staff time and resources caused by the training and retraining of their replacements.

The job of a leader in that situation is to remove barriers for someone to do his or her best work. Businesses have learned to do conduct "exit" interviews when people decide to leave. If you wish to find out why people are leaving, conduct an exit interview. If a number of people respond with similar answers, determine whether the problems can be fixed. Conversely, you might not want to wait until someone announces plans to leave. Instead, proactively conduct a "stay" interview and ask them the following:

- What can I do to remove obstacles in order to help you do your job better?
- How can I help you succeed?
- What areas of our school need improvement?
- What things inhibit you from working at your best?
- What things should be measured to show we are making improvements?

Education today is losing talented, bright, capable young men and women who are leaving teaching in sizable numbers, shifting their lives from the classrooms and the front offices into jobs that are less stressful, pay more, and are more appreciated. While there is always a steady ebb and flow of young people into and out of the field of education, the ongoing drain of experienced and bright young people after three, four, or five years is a concern. As a leader, take time during the school day, throughout the year, to recognize and appreciate the people who work for you—not just the teachers but also the dietitians, bus drivers, and those who clean the school. Everyone needs to feel valued. Compliment people when they do something particularly well. Do not assume that anyone is above the need for encouragement. That includes the staff, students, parents, school resource officers, and police.

Use social media to get messages out to staff, parents, and teachers. Take the opportunity to say nice things to others. They appreciate it.

New teachers can feel frustrated, overwhelmed, and angry by the strain of work. Be aware and sensitive about how staff members are feeling. Send e-mail birthday, anniversary, and sympathy cards when appropriate.

What are the purposes of classroom observations? They should not be seen as a "gotcha" moment. Encourage colleagues to observe one another. Observations need not be announced in advance. In order to ensure that evaluators view a typical lesson, observations should not be scheduled. Evaluators need to view what normally occurs in a teacher's classroom, not lessons and activities that have been specially prepared for the observation.

Continue to grow as a professional. When you read a book, whether fiction or nonfiction, that you enjoy, share it with the faculty via a discussion or blog. Encourage members of the faculty to do something similar. Start a staff educational library if one does not already exist. What skills or areas of professional knowledge do you need to strengthen?

New Leaders

Over the past several years, there has been a growing sense of urgency by national, state, and local education agencies to deepen and strengthen the candidate pool of promising educational leaders, recruit them into leadership positions, and retain their services by supporting and helping them improve their leadership skills. Internationally, trends suggest an ever-increasing shortage of individuals who possess leadership potential that can be cultivated to effectively lead and manage schools in the twenty-first century. Traditionally, educational leaders have come from the teaching ranks and follow a conventional career path into leadership positions, as observed by Susan Gates and others in their report *Who Is Leading Our Schools*. In most educational systems, there are no specific criteria by which individuals are identified as having leadership potential. Often, individuals seek leadership positions through self-selection, sometimes accompanied by encouragement from supervisors based on perceived leadership ability.

More Thoughts on Leadership

- Educators do not need to be motivated; they naturally are. That is why they chose to be educators. However, after about six years they can become unmotivated. We need to identify what has unmotivated them and remove those factors.

- Developing management skills is hard for everyone; it is about making mistakes, about trial and error.

- The best way to inspire people is when they see you doing what they have done or when you are in the trenches with them.

- Set expectations for staff—knowing that there is a fine line between inspiring people and setting expectations so high that they cannot be reached.

- Respect the people who were there before you came. Come in with all these great ideas, but not as if you know it all, or you will not get them to buy in.

- Be decisive. People see signs of weakness. People will find a hole if any exist—and even if there are none.

- Ask, "What do I need to get better at?"

- You need to have passion for what you do and compassion for people.

- Ask, "What should I know about you that I haven't asked? What are three areas of self-improvement that you are working on?

- You need to spend time working on things that are not working.

- Make yourself available to people; they will tell you what they think.

- Eat with the staff and move around. Do not always sit with the same people.

- Be positive. Praise people when things are going well.

- Ask, "What would you do in this situation?"

- Be very clear about what you expect from people. Meet with them regularly. Help keep them on track.

- Any good leader sets up a system to ensure that critical information reaches the top of the chain. There are different ways of communication. The purposes are to inform, provide feedback, and motivate. Open as many lines of communication as possible. Support and be open to different points of view.

Failure. Recognize when people take a risk. Do not penalize failure. David Gangel, former superintendent of the Rappahannock County School System in Virginia, stated: "We have never been taught how to deal with failure. Therefore, when it occurs, we freeze." "Many people, educators, students and parents, are not accustomed to encounter any kinds of roadblocks or disappointments that often come with making hard choices. Students have unrealistic expectations in dealing with failure or learning from adverse experiences. They have not been taught the coping skills." But failure is a wonderful teacher; it teaches you what not to do the next time. People probably learn just as much from failure as they do from success.

Working hard is not the criterion if you do not achieve. I have heard students say, "I really worked hard," and I have had to reply, "But you didn't pass." However, if students are permitted not only chances to fail but also direction toward doing better, then yes, they can learn. In small groups, Dr. Laurence G. Weinzimmer said, "They want you to believe the sky is always blue and the road is always smooth, but the sky is not always blue, and the road is not always smooth. What we found with most of our interviews was that most leaders told us the most important lessons came from their toughest challenges, not from imitating somebody else's success." To quote a motivational saying, "Never let success get to your head. Never let failure get to your heart." As the legendary National Football League coach Don Shula put it, "I didn't get consumed by losses, and I didn't get overwhelmed by successes." Promote the good things that are happening. Ensure that people see the positive things while not ignoring the negatives.

Leaders Helping Teachers

Good things are happening in all schools, but are these things aligned to the school, district, state, and federal goals of education?

It is your job to be honest. You have a responsibility to make sure the school is succeeding, for if you do not, no one will.

Coaches/Mentors. Select highly effective and experienced teachers as coaches or mentors to new teachers. They should be chosen based on their record of advancing student achievement and their ability to work with adults. Insofar as possible, coaches should be matched with teachers by grade and/or subject. Furthermore, new teachers should have the opportunity to provide feedback on a coach or mentor's performance.

Observations. Suggest that new teachers observe accomplished teachers. New teachers often say the most beneficial aspect of starting out is having the opportunity to observe more accomplished teachers. Opportunities for peer observation should be frequent throughout a teacher's first year, provided the individual school or district can implement a program that will add real value. The problem with observation programs such as these is that strong principals will know whom the new teachers should observe, but weaker principals will not know this as well. For a program like this to work, some district coordination is necessary, particularly in order to intervene in schools with weaker leadership. Superintendents should provide incentives to accomplish this.

All teachers—not just new ones—should be observed frequently, and by more than one person. Principals, their designees, peer reviewers, and occasionally third-party observers working for the central office can and should observe all teachers, both tenured and untenured. Not all feedback need be formal. Many principals find it helpful to make brief but frequent visits to classrooms, jotting down a few quick notes to discuss with the teacher later. Especially at the secondary level, observers may need to follow several linked lessons to see how a teacher is faring. Having subject matter specialists observe teachers for the content of their lessons is particularly important.

Protocols that incorporate multiple observers' reflections permit the district to assess the robustness of an individual principal's ratings, measured against those of other observers. Correlation of findings may reduce concerns over the arbitrary nature of evaluations, as teachers rightfully perceive the single-observer evaluation as being prone to bias or favoritism.

If the school has a teacher's union, ask the union leader or a designee if he or she would be willing to be part of an observation team.

Struggling Teachers. Any teacher with identified deficiencies needs to receive support as soon as possible. The frequency of evaluation of nontenured teachers increases the likelihood that struggling teachers will not go unrecognized. However, principals must ensure that tenured teachers also receive immediate support; the option to place a tenured teacher in remediation during a three-year cycle should be used more frequently, and intervention should begin as soon as instructional deficiencies are noted.

Teachers who do not improve in three years should be eligible for dismissal. It generally takes three years to master teaching. Yet some people cannot master the profession in that time period. Nontenured teachers with unsatisfactory performance should not have their contract renewed for the following year. Tenured teachers who receive two unsatisfactory evaluations in five years should be eligible for dismissal. The poorly performing teacher who continues to be rated unsatisfactory after remediation should be considered for dismissal in the same year.

The district should support principals in dismissing ineffective teachers. Principals should receive early and significant support from the district with regard to underperforming teachers. Such support should include an outside observation by a district observer. Keep an extensive record of assistance offered, because records are especially critical should dismissal become necessary.

The Best Parts

Encourage people by helping them find mentors. One of the best mentors I ever had was Russell Ackoff. He used an analogy that went something like this: "There are 150 car manufacturers around the world. Let us say that we wanted to build the best car possible. So we took the best parts of a Honda, Toyota, Hyundai, General Motors, Ford, etc., and put them together. Would we have the best car? Of course not! It is not the best parts that make the best organizations or products but the interaction of those parts." In education, how do we put the best parts together?

Dr. Myron Tribus came up with a list of elements of a high-performing school:

- Aim
- Philosophy
- Vision—what does success look like?
- Strategy

- Provided resources (time, money)

- Reward system

- Organization

- Involved constituencies

Simplifying the complex is an administrator's job. When giving speeches, be concise, be brief, and then be gone. Otherwise, listeners will have trouble identifying the core points. In delivering workshops, I ask myself, "What are the three things I want people to leave the room knowing?" Synthesize.

Not everything you do will work, so you need how to handle adversity. Some people know how to deal with adversity better than others. Some people embrace it, while others abhor it. Some people work better under pressure.

Why do some people succeed while others do not? Some of my friends cite "intelligence." Not so. As observed by Richard Nisbett, a professor of psychology at the University of Michigan, it is not how much intelligence people have but rather how it is used.

Focus on doing the job you have, not the job you want to have in the future. Be really good at what you do.

Learn how to delegate. Learn how to let go. Do not micromanage. Avoiding micromanagement is critical. Let people do their job. If they are not doing their job, then you have the wrong people doing the work. Identify choke points that slow down improvement.

The finish line is the beginning of a whole new race.

At the beginning, I felt if people were successful, they were fine. This was not good. The role of a supervisor is to facilitate and create an environment where everyone can be successful.

Benchmarking Leaders

Do not believe your own press. Know both your strengths and weakness. We all have weaknesses. Form a team to overcome them.

Some people achieve leadership positions, by various means, but they are not true leaders. They lack vision.

Educators must be both the manager, of things, and a leader, of people. It is difficult to be both. People can describe to you what it means to be a school leader, but until you become one, it is not what you anticipated. People are looking to you for guidance, wanting your time and anticipating your expertise.

Behave consistently, but do not become rigid. Consistent behavior results in a clear understanding by others what to expect from you and what you expect from them. Like pilots, school leaders cannot afford to have a bad day.

Prioritize

Football coach Bear Bryant told his players, "When you get to the end zone, act like you've been there before." Robert Fuller: "Common language leads to common knowledge, leads to common practice." Dr. Jerry Goolsby, associate professor of marketing, University of South Florida: "Every system is designed to get the results it produces."

School administrators (principals, superintendents) are given many balls to juggle. When juggling balls, they need to determine which are made of glass and which are made of rubber. Educators are frequently forced to deal with crises without the ability to plan. You need to measure the amount of time spent compared to the "return on investment." Know the answer to the following question: "Is this really a good use of my time?" The question can be answered by measuring the impact of the effort. As supreme commander of Allied forces in Western Europe during World War II, General Dwight D. Eisenhower needed to make a huge number of decisions. He developed a chart to help him handle them. By using this template, he was able to divide the decisions into those that were both urgent and important, urgent but not important, important but not urgent, and neither urgent nor important. Not everything in your inbox is urgent or important. How can you use this matrix to help deal with making decisions?

At my workshops, I ask people, "What is the greatest challenge you face?" and uniformly they say "time"—"We don't have enough time." The workload of the job appears to be constantly increasing, along with the accountability and responsibility of schools. Tasks that formerly were the responsibility of parents, families, or religious institutions, from teaching driving and swimming to teaching values, such as not to use drugs or alcohol or not to have sex, have been reassigned to schools. This is in addition to the traditional responsibilities such as preparing students in reading, math, and science. All of this has been done without any additional preparation of educators or time added.

There are endless distractions and disruptions: e-mails, phone calls, parental requests, and people who expect immediate answers to their questions. What do you deal with first, people or things? You need to prioritize. I was taught to use three-by-five index cards to develop a to-do list. On one side of a card, which was easy to carry, I put the things that I had to do for the day, and on the other, the phone calls I needed to make. I then prioritized by putting numbers next to the calls and things I needed to do. Priority went to those calls and other things to do that would yield the greatest return.

Despite time constraints, take time to decompress and smell the roses. I used to walk around the building away from my office and the telephone. Everyone needs some time to think. People need to know that you have a life outside of school.

Who Will Teach Our Teachers to Teach Our Kids?

Educators, politicians, and businesspeople all agree that leadership in education has never been more critical for public school systems. They also share a grave concern about the looming shortage of qualified educational leaders.

On October 2, 2000, the headline on the cover of *Newsweek* cover read, "Who Will Teach Our Kids?" The accompanying article projected that over the next ten years, 2.2 million teachers—of the existing workforce of 2.6 million—would leave the profession because of retirement, low pay, low morale, frustration with the educational system, and better opportunities elsewhere.

Yet the crisis is not limited to just teachers. According to an article in *USA Today*, "Roughly half of the nation's superintendents are older than age 50 and will likely leave their jobs in the next five years. . . . Those officials worry that there are not enough qualified candidates to fill the vacancies."

The article went on to quote Mary Lee Fitzgerald, director of education programs for the Wallace–Reader's Digest Fund: "The principalship is a bull market. Nobody wants the job. Modest pay, long hours, uneven resources, problematic authority, increased expectations of the public make this job in a competitive market a no-winner for the top half of the class."

The job of school superintendent is often the least stable position in the school district. Tenure averages just thirty-six months (less in our inner-city school districts). According to the Council of the Great City Schools in Washington, D.C., "The average tenure of the current Great City School superintendent increased from $2\frac{1}{2}$ years in 2001 to $2\frac{3}{4}$ years in 2003. The majority of superintendents (54 percent) have been in office one to five years. Approximately 31 percent . . . have been in office for one year or less. Only 15 percent . . . had five or more years in their current position." However, a superintendent must learn the culture of the district, develop a strategic plan for school improvement, and then deploy that plan—a difficult, if not impossible, task to accomplish in three years or less.

A New Population of Students

An article by Forrest J. Troy noted that, according to the U.S. Department of Education, our nation has about 87,000 schools in more than 14,000 districts and approximately 46.3 million students in public school classrooms. More than 6.2 million children have limited English proficiency; 2 million speak no English. Two million latchkey children go home to an empty house; another two million endure abuse and neglect at home. An estimated 1 million children suffer from the effects of lead poisoning, a major cause of slow learning; more than 500,000 come from foster and institutional care; 30,000 are products of fetal alcohol syndrome. Nearly 400,000 were crack babies and are the children of other drug users. More than half a million are homeless, lacking a permanent address. Of children younger than eighteen, approximately 20 percent (14.4 million) come from homes with extreme poverty. More than half of poor children are white and live in rural and suburban areas. And America's schools are taking in growing minority populations from countries that lack strong educational infrastructures.

Principals and superintendents must respond to a host of new or added challenges: diversity of cultural backgrounds, waves of immigration, income disparities, physical and mental disabilities, and variation in learning capability. Increasingly, schools must adapt to address the needs of at-risk, nontraditional learners. Wherever teacher education programs have not kept pace with these challenges, many of their graduates must learn on the job, under the tutelage of their school leaders. And the tasks of scheduling, programming, ensuring security, and providing counseling have all become more complex.

When Henry Ford's company sold its first cars, he famously stated, "You can have any color you want as long as it's black." Ford's plants were set up accordingly. Ford Motor Company could not address the needs of today's public if it were still offering only one choice. Similarly, schools can no longer afford to offer one-size-fits-all education; today's society demands an individualized approach that caters to the needs of each child. Today's educational leaders cannot rely solely on traditional methods of teaching and learning; they need a new repertoire of skills and approaches.

Don't Be Afraid of Aiming High

Henry Ford is credited with saying, "If you think you can or if you think you can't, you will be right." Have faith in what you do. If school leadership is a challenge you think you will relish, go for it. It is the best job in the school. It is not easy, but it offers you the opportunity to make a difference on a scale unlike any you have known.

Teacher Unions. Teacher unions do not hire teachers. Giving three to five years to gain tenure, after which teachers can be let go only for "cause" using due process, allows the individual time to gain footing and learn how to implement the teaching process. Involve the union, if it exists. The union leader can preempt problems by coming in and letting you know if the staff or a member of the staff was unsettled about something. Do not perceive unions as "the enemy within"; they can play a constructive and supportive role if the in-school leadership-union relationship is based on mutual respect.

Bill Daggett has said there needs to be three elements for school success: "rigor, relevance and relationships and the most important of these is relationships." Leaders need to build relationships with teachers, parents, children, and community stakeholders.

Having a school leader with vision is important. Having a school leader who knows how to translate that vision into reality is even more important. Turning around a school or school system in the absence of effective school leadership is impossible.

Develop a clear vision, and do not lose faith in it.

CHAPTER 4
School Culture

"Culture eats change for lunch."
—attributed to **Peter Drucker**

Current data indicate that increasing numbers of youngsters are not being served by the schools they attend. Many schools have examined their school culture, found them wanting, and made changes. Unfortunately, the data indicate that far more needs to be done. School culture needs to support teachers, student learning, parents, and families.

Scores of metaphors have been used to describe the complexity and ever-changing nature of school cultures, but one of the most descriptive, and appropriate, is Rick DuFour and Becky Burnette's metaphor of school culture as a garden. Like a garden, a school's culture is always changing; it is dynamic and in constant need of care. Tending to culture is nonlinear and requires rapid responses to unanticipated problems as they arise. A school's culture is influenced by both external and internal factors. A garden, too, is affected by internal and external factors. The most vital elements occur underground and are not readily visible. Indeed, like a garden, if left untended a school's culture degenerates into a disheveled mess of weeds and waste where little, if any, of the original crop ever makes it to maturity and bears fruit. In such instances, it is imperative that the gardeners—the school leaders and staff—are intimately aware of what they are trying to grow so that they know the proper kind and amount of nutrients, herbicides, pesticides, and watering to use. It is important to note that with the proper amount of fertilizer, any garden can flourish . . . but too much can kill everything. It is the role of the staff to plant the seeds of learning, and culture can achieve that end.

Defining School Culture

John Siskind, past director of alternative education at Winston-Salem/ Forsyth County Schools, North Carolina, stated:

- Every school has a culture.

- In every school/district, the leader sets the direction.

- Principals/superintendents need to hire professional staff who support the school culture they envision.

Accepting that every school has its own culture even means that a school across the street from a high-performing school, with the same pool of parents, students, and staff, may not be high performing too. A school culture does not just appear. It starts slowly and evolves over time. It influences the people who work in the schools every day. It is guided by leaders and adopted by teachers and staff. But often it is an ongoing, collaborative effort that ebbs and flows against the daily operation of a school or district. Initially it is the role of the school leader to determine the culture of the school and the way its teachers and staff interact with parents, students, and the community. School values and policies are most often informal and are established during the early life of the school. The leader's own approach and behavior are often reflected in the general behavior of the school's working staff. As the school matures, it becomes necessary to formally define and clearly communicate the organization's cultural values and the behavior expected from its employees. The school principal's leadership style is often based on previous educational and personal experiences. Some of the leader's values and characteristics become rules that the staff follows. These values form the basis of the school's culture and can become important factors that generate long-term performance. The school's culture is its brand. What is the cultural brand of your school? Is it a "good" school? A fair school? Or a "bad" school to work in? What will be the reaction of your staff to a new strategy for changing its culture? Your school has its strategic plan. Does it have a culture strategy in place? Educators are loyal to their school's culture, not to any new strategy. Existing strategies provide stability and assure more of the same.

School performance is determined by its culture and the topics concerning school improvement. Webster's defines "culture" as the integrated pattern of human behavior that includes thought, speech, action, and artifacts and depends upon humans' capacity for learning and transmitting knowledge to succeeding generations. Continuous learning is the new normal.

Understanding that to change one part of the culture frequently impacts many or all other parts is critical to know if one is to successfully implement change. The law of unintended consequences states that any purposeful action will produce some unintended consequences. Changing one part of a school organization will impact other parts of a school organization in unforeseen ways. It is amazing how many times educators try to change the school culture without realizing that they are really trying to change human behavior.

"To manage a system effectively, you might focus on the interactions of the parts rather than their behavior taken separately."
—Dr. Russell Ackoff

Human behavior, particularly when it has become part of daily, monthly, and yearly ritual, is extremely difficult to change. Schools are, by and large, a system of human behaviors that have been set in stone by daily ritual and habit and that often span years—even generations. Knowing that a culture includes how people think, speak, and act, and those things that they create because of their thoughts and actions, is necessary to understanding culture. A school leader must also understand that both failure and success in changing a school culture lie in the effective understanding and use of these very aspects. Understood in this definition is that thought, speech, and action, and even the creation of artifacts, come from individual and group belief.

Richard Elmore theorized that to change a school culture, we must first change human behavior. Dr. Elmore states that one cannot will, dictate, command, or even cajole change, but that only by changing human behavior, tasks, and rituals can we hope to impact change in the school culture. First change the faculty's habits, he says, and gradually the culture will change when people see the benefits of the change in their practice. If a culture is dependent on the ability to create order and stability, then it stands to reason that trying to change the existing culture goes against people's natural ability to sustain the very culture they helped to build. Change is a threat to what has become the norm, and by human nature it will be resisted. If the school experiences a great deal of teacher and administrator turnover, important elements of the culture may be lost.

There are three truths that we want to examine as we look at school culture as an integrated pattern.

1. Schools, like all human endeavors, are complex systems in which one part of the system is linked to another.

2. Schools, like all systems, have structures that have been built by scaffolding one structure onto another over time.

3. Schools, unlike other systems, have more emotional strings attached because the well-being of children is inextricably tied to the success or failure of the systems.

The school principal who fails to understand these simple but potent truths will fail in attempts to alter the system to improve the culture. Principals with good intentions have been surprised to find that one small change can bring many concerns from multiple stakeholders. Most often, the reason for this concern is that educators understand that one change begets many others, because school systems are so linked. For example, a principal who decides that since most core subjects are taught in the morning, announcements should occur at the end of the day, rather than at the beginning, may have a concerned coach, music teacher, cafeteria manager, parent, and librarian all at his or her office door. This is a simple example, but if every change attempted by the leader is met with challenges from multiple camps, much time will be lost, and little change will occur. The effective leader understands that what appears to be a simple change is always more complex. Because schools have systems that are built one structure onto another over time, to impact one part of the structure is to impact several parts. Planning, collaboration, and dedication to the change are necessary for any real change to occur. One must also be ready to deal with collateral damage that is not expected because of the change. It will always happen and must always be expected.

Paradigm Shift and Resistance to Change

Any change can engender a reflexive resistance from those being asked to change. That resistance, in part, is a product of trying to change paradigms. Joel Barker describes paradigms as the lens through which we see things. In other words, our personal histories and experiences color our view of reality and help define what is seen as the right way to do things. Any attempted changing of a paradigm is often seen as being antithetical to "the way we do things." The paradigms associated with public education are some of the strongest in existence because they were formed, and continually reinforced, during the formative years of schools. It should come as no surprise that such paradigms are very hard to change. However, the paradigms surrounding education are further strengthened by the belief that things were "so much better yesterday."

Why Do We Do Things That Way?

In most of today's schools, staff and administrative turnover is a given. Statistics indicate that somewhere between 35 and 45 percent of all teachers leave the profession within their first five years. The constant turnover, or churn, has resulted in schools where many students have been there longer than many of their teachers. In such schools, there is often little understanding of why things are done in a particular way. "That's the way it's always been done around here." Unfortunately, that is the only reason many can give to explain the hows and whys of their school's culture. In such instances, it is far more likely that the school's culture is simply the product of decisions made because they were expeditious, not because they were appropriate. Both students and teachers deserve better. Change in education requires risk taking—but many schools would rather succeed in doing nothing than failing by doing something.

Why do we do things that way? Regardless of the answer, "that way" is usually seen as the proper way. Such beliefs are the primary reason that reculturing a school is accepted as being extremely challenging. Though that may be true, it is also true that school cultures are continuously changing. For school leaders, the question then becomes, "Do you want to guide the change, or be a slave to it?" Sometimes, beginning the process of reculturing requires only a small step.

Too often, leaders who are well intentioned begin culture change by approaching that which is intangible, but most important. This approach seems to make sense because the most important elements to change are very often those things that cannot be touched or seen. Really believing that all children can learn, that the adults in the building need to be learners, and that the parents want what is best for their children are all beliefs that must exist in a positive school culture. But leaders will find that changing the unseen is far more difficult than changing those things that are visible and concrete. As the quotes above indicate, these leaders choose instead to improve the visible. We solve visible symptoms rather than the deeper underlying causes. Letting everyone experience physical change in the building is a great way to say, "Things are going to be different, better, around here!" The wise leader will get everyone's attention by changing the visible and concrete while working on the intangible. One must caution, however, that far too many leaders spend much energy and effort in changing the concrete and never move to the important changes needed in the intangible. Painting the building does not improve student achievement.

School culture is complicated. The school leader who overlooks the complexity of culture when trying to implement change is certain to fail. The successful leader understands that school culture is created by scaffolding patterns over time. These patterns are tightly integrated, tied to human behavior, including how people think, speak, and act. People create artifacts that represent the culture. The culture continues if people continue to transmit it from generation to generation. This very idea of transmission of the culture makes it more difficult to change. This transmission may also lead to people not understanding why certain things in the culture exist, but simply accepting them as "the norm."

How educators "see" students ultimately determines how they treat them. If we believe that students are different, we treat them differently—and they become different. Society and schools have put labels on children (to name a few: AHDH, "slow," special education, alternative learners, low performing, disabled, incorrigible). As a result, we may first see the label rather than the child. I once visited an alternative school to speak to a group of "socially maladjusted" (their terminology) youngsters. A group of sixth, seventh, and eighth grade youngsters who had been labeled as uneducable were marched into the room by two staff members. One was at the front of the group and the other brought up the rear, as if they were guarding prisoners who were being marched to a meal and might escape. The only thing they lacked were T-shirts indicating that they were "losers." The body language of the youngsters indicated that they did not want to be there, and they were openly hostile at the whole process. Obviously, they had been briefed to behave for their school's guest. I asked a series of questions and played a number of involvement games. The longer I engaged them, the more they relaxed and became involved. There were seventeen of these students, and they worked with us for a little more than an hour. Admittedly, there is a *big* difference in working with these youngsters for a whole day, a week, or a school year. We started talking about what they saw as their future. They wanted to be basketball players, singers, lawyers, doctors—but they were coming to the realization that might never happen. One young lady was sullen and withdrawn, basically uncooperative and unresponsive. After the session, we found out that her parents had split up and she had been placed in a foster home. By the end of the session, we had discovered that these were bright young people who simply had been "disconnected"—disconnected from school, frequently disconnected from their families, and often disconnected from society.

The director then took me on a tour of the building. Proudly, she showed off the computer labs, and we observed several teachers at work. As we walked around, we found ourselves outside a classroom with one of the staff members who had brought the group to see us. We asked jokingly, "What are you guarding?" He said that it was the classroom for the students we had met. (We were not invited to go into it.) We were told that a curriculum was in the process of being developed, but none presently existed. The students were given busy work to do and were isolated from the rest of the student population. The only way we can describe it was that it was isolation from the general population, just as prisons isolate the "most dangerous" from the general prison population. They had been removed because they were disruptive and inhibited the learning of others. We do not have a problem with removing disruptive students so that others can learn. But educators need to identify why students are disruptive. So far as we can tell, no one had identified the "whys." We failed to ask what their parents feel about the situation. Maybe the parents are unable to handle their child's behavior and conduct and have left that up to the school system to address their needs. We isolate, segregate, and separate students who do not fit into the existing system, which exists in different environments. Increasingly, schools are dealing with growing numbers of nontraditional students who come from nontraditional homes and learn in nontraditional ways. The reality is that traditional teaching and learning techniques do not work with nontraditional students, and we cannot use such techniques with such students. If we want to reach these youngsters, we must use nontraditional techniques. Most educators come from traditional families. (two-parent homes, a stay-at-home mom, with a value placed on education as a way up in society). The students who are most likely to succeed in school are traditional students. But nontraditional students, like the rest of us, have strengths as well as weaknesses. It is easy to identify their weaknesses. (They come from single-parent, female-dominated homes, they live in poverty, they speak English as a second language, etc.) How many of us can identify their strengths?

Toxicity

Wikipedia defines toxicity as "the degree to which something is able to produce illness or damage to an exposed organism." Toxicity can, and often does, refer to the effect on a whole organism. By extension, the word may be metaphorically used to describe toxic effects on larger and more complex groups, such as the family unit or society at large.

How do you know if schools are toxic? Many educators believe and tell you, "I know it when I see it." Sometimes this is true. One can walk into a toxic school and see the lack of pride in the dirt on the floor or the graffiti on the walls or the smell in the student bathrooms. Toxic school cultures can and will destroy the most well-meaning leadership. Not only are students forced to go into toxic environments, but so are educators. How do you measure toxicity? One way is by the number of teachers leaving or by the churn among school administrators. Here are some of the ways of identifying a school's toxicity:

- Autocratic administrator
- Oppressive environment
    ° For students
    ° For parents
    ° For staff
- Dirty building (floors, cafeteria, bathrooms, perimeter of building)
- High number of absences (staff, students)
- High churn of teachers, staff, and administrators
- Lack of transparency in making decisions

Thankfully, the percentage of schools that are truly toxic is small. However, many other schools exhibit signs of toxicity in any of four areas:

- Student learning
- Students

- Parents
- Educational staff

Toxicity to Student Learning. Schools profess that learning is most important, but students are pulled out of classes with regularity for outside activities such as plays, rehearsals, and practice for sporting events, rather than having these events take place before or after classes or on the weekend.

Although student learning is most important, the school showcases contain only athletic awards. Athletes are given jackets, trophies, and receptions to honor their achievements, while student achievement and scholarship are largely ignored.

Although student learning is most important, endless, sometimes mindless, announcements are made on the public-address system, interrupting instruction.

Student work is not shown in the halls or in classrooms. Rather, commercial posters are placed around the building. This is equally true for high schools as it is for middle and elementary schools. Hallways in healthy schools should be extensions of the classrooms; a place where exceptional student work is celebrated.

Toxicity to Students. Bullying is ignored rather than prevented, and bullies are not punished.

Students are not treated equally. While the school professes to treat all students equally, athletes or members of the student government are given privileges denied to the bulk of the student population. Inequitable and unfair dispensation of discipline is consistently cited by dropouts as a primary reason they decided to leave school.

Students ditch classes with regularity, while the school ignores the behavior.

Failing classes and examinations are ignored, and the school does not identify the causes of failure.

Toxicity to Parents. Parents are not represented on any committees affecting learning. For example, they are not put on the school improvement committee.

Parents are used only for fund-raising or the collection of funds at football games but not as volunteers to help students read or to relieve teachers of nonteaching responsibilities.

The Parents Teacher Organization does not have representation based on the ethnicity of the student population, and the school does not make any effort to recruit ethnic representation into the organization.

Parent meetings are held at inconvenient times so that parents are unable to attend. No attempts are made to find out when most parents can attend the meetings.

Although the school has students and parents who speak languages other than English, no attempt is made to send announcements home in a language other than English.

While the school is aware that students have younger siblings, no attempt is made to provide child care when parents are asked to come to school for meetings.

The only phone calls made to homes criticize student performance, while no attempt is made to compliment parents for positive student behavior and performance.

Parents' experience or knowledge is not tapped to aid the school.

Toxicity to Educational Staff. Counselors are overburdened with paperwork that can be given to aides to do. They spend less time counseling and more time filling out forms or programming students.

Teachers transfer to other schools with great regularity. No attempt is made to find out why.

New teachers are not mentored and are not given any assistance by the administration. If assistance is given, it is little more than linking the new teacher with a "mentor" who has merely been at the school for a while. This "mentor" usually has no idea of how-to mentor, has no training in mentoring, and is appointed without choice.

New teachers are assigned to the lowest-performing students.

New teachers are placed in temporary buildings with the belief "out of sight, out of mind."

Positive vs. Negative School Cultures

If one subscribes to the definition of culture in this book, then one begins to understand the difficulty of transforming a negative school culture into a positive one. In his book *Good to Great*, Jim Collins states that the job of a leader should be to "make sure that the right people are on the bus, that they are seated in the right seats, and that the wrong people are kicked off the bus." In a civil service, union-protected, nonprofit environment, this is very difficult to do. How do you "kick off the bus" tenured teachers who are simply waiting for retirement? How do you encourage parents to become involved in school when their primary concerns are feeding, housing, and clothing their families?

Because everyone has gone to school, everyone believes he or she has the answers to what ails education. Educational policy is primarily not made by the professionals in the field but by politicians who look for quick solutions to complex problems. Parents and businesspeople all want input into the educational process but, in many cases, base that input upon antiquated and outmoded paradigms.

Negative Begets Negative. It stands to reason that if school cultures have systems that are built by scaffolding one structure onto another over time, then negative cultures are built by scaffolding negative structures onto another over time. A policy that negatively impacts the learning environment is likely to negatively impact the attitudes of those who value learning in the school. This impact may create negative feelings in those who value learning toward those who made the negative policy. School administrators need to address negative attitudes held by staff and those who promulgate it. Negative begets negative. If left to scaffold unabated, the negatives become the school culture. Integrated systems are connected, and to tamper with one part impacts many others. Unfortunately, the removal of one negative part of the school culture does not start a chain reaction that removes all others. Negative cultures are highly integrated and are certainly tied to human behavior at its worst. Negative school cultures create negative artifacts, negative attitudes, negative speech, and negative thoughts.

Negative Is as Negative Does. As noted above, Richard Elmore's research indicates that one must change human behavior first before attempting to change the culture. The leader who understands this idea is more likely to understand that one must not only dream of a more positive culture but expect that there will be one. Part of the expectation is that the people in the culture will behave in a way that supports positive outcomes. The school leader who allows negative speech, thoughts, and attitudes to continue is one who really does not expect the culture to become more positive. Certainly, this is not to say that the leader can command a positive culture and expect it to appear. But no leader can expect to help develop a positive school culture if negative attributes can flourish and grow.

One of my mentors, Dr. Myron Tribus, came to my school and met with a group of African American students. He was disturbed when the students looked down in response to his questions. He asked, "Why don't you look me in the eye when you respond?" A student responded, "When you look someone in the eye in our community, it encourages confrontation." Dr. Tribus did not understand that that was part of a minority, inner-city culture. Educators need to bridge the various gaps that exist between classes, cultures, and ethnicities. It is a difficult task, and training is needed. Changing a school's culture is the hardest part of any transformation. If you do not change the organization's culture, you will fail trying to change anything. Trying to change an organization's culture takes time, and school leaders need to develop patience to make that happen. Leaders need people who will tell them things they may not want to hear. It takes a long time to build a shared vision and avoid toxic cultures. Dr. Tribus once told me that "changing a school's culture is like trying to get the dead to move the cemetery."

The hardest words in the English language are "I made a mistake." In many schools, educators are afraid to admit they made a mistake. They are afraid they will be reprimanded, or even fired. Schools need to create a culture where people feel safe to bring their problems. If you change schools, you will find that each school has a different culture, and you will need to earn the trust of the staff. The key to changing a school's culture is to have an open, transparent environment.

When I became a supervisor at a school that was a prime example of a churn factory, I inherited several teachers who came from different schools with different cultures. Most of them were excellent, but others were poisoning the rest and the culture of the school. These people may have been fair or good teachers, but they acted as saboteurs to the mission and vision in that they did not work well with others, especially the new teachers. They were insidious in attempting to erode the school's culture and were determined to undermine fellow teachers. Schools are gossip mills, and they thrived on gossip that spread malicious and often untrue stories. The school's administrators—principals and assistant principals— left with regularity. The faculty members felt they had been abandoned. The school was run by the "ad hoc committee," a group of anonymous individuals who sabotaged any change they did not like or approve of. One told me, "That's not the way we did it in my old school." They had a different culture from the one I was trying to develop. But they also are going to tell you all the things wrong with what you are doing and what is wrong with everyone else. They believed that their beliefs were correct and everything contrary to those beliefs was wrong. At meetings, they accepted what had been discussed but then held after-meeting meetings where they criticized the decisions that had just been made. They were comfortable with the status quo and wanted more people to join them in supporting it. When something went right, they took the credit whether they were responsible or not. When something went wrong, it was always somebody else's fault. Not only did they not want to do more; they wanted others to do less. You need to explain that new cultures bring in new ideas and new ways of doing things. Educators do not spend enough time communicating with one another.

Instructors operate in different silos, and there are so many silos. School cultures tend to isolate people rather than to bring them together. Teachers teach alone, develop lesson plans alone, develop and give their own tests. They are in their rooms alone. Many develop their own tests, lesson plans, and curricula. At best, they speak to other people in their own grade or, in middle and high schools, in their own subject area. Teachers spend most of their days in isolation from other adults. This is especially true in elementary classrooms, where educators spend their entire day with young people. Leaders need to break down these silos, because we all work in a school *system*. Educators need to create an environment where teachers are working with other teachers, sharing and building knowledge and best practices.

Build Staff Pride and School Spirit

Educators need to have pride in themselves, their profession, and their school. School and district administrators need to train people to take pride in their building. Schools need to be friendly places not only for students and their families but for teachers, staff, and principals. By building pride, educators will get teachers to want to remain, not resign.

Staff should be able to provide answers to the following questions:

- What is the school doing well?
- Why do these things work?
- What needs to be improved?
- How do we get what makes things work, to make the improvements?
- What things do we have to measure to show that we are improving?

Teachers should hang signs outside their classrooms indicating the schools they graduated from, just as doctors and lawyers hang evidence of where they attended and graduated from.

At George Westinghouse High School, where I was a school administrator, we created a bulletin board of the positive news about staff announcing weddings, the births of children and grandchildren, graduations. The work can include positive news about faculty, such as their participation in out-of-school events or their achieving advanced degrees.

Hang graphs of student achievements. Graphs showing improvements in testing or attendance can be placed in visible locations around the building. The graph lines should be going up, not down. Graphs should emphasize the positive, not the negative. (For example, you want to show the number of students who graduate, not those who drop out.)

Celebrate school successes. Find occasions to celebrate the success of students, whether in academics or sports or student activities, and give credit to teachers and coaches.

Hang pictures of new staff in staff rooms and the staff dining room to make them feel that they are a member of the school. Introduce them a faculty meeting.

Train students to take pride in their building.

Students cannot be expected to learn in an environment that is toxic. Teachers cannot be expected to teach in a school that is toxic. How do we measure toxicity? Are the students and staff safe? Is the learning environment friendly to parents as well as students? Can your staff identify the culture of the school? Do they believe that *all* students can learn? That parents are important to the learning process, and that the school is a learning institution as well as a teaching institution?

PART III
REFRESHING

CHAPTER 5

Refreshing the Current Staff

"It's too bad that the people who really know how to run the country are too busy teaching school."
—Anonymous

We are living in a rapidly changing world. Our present teaching staff is dealing with a growing number of nontraditional students, who come from nontraditional families and learn in nontraditional ways. The vast majority of teachers in classrooms need to be trained in how to deal with these nontraditional students. As Abigail Geiger recently pointed out, research indicates that the majority of students now in classrooms are nonwhite, but the majority of teachers are white. A compilation of education statistics by Maya Riser-Kositsky for Education Week noted that as of 2015, 48.9 percent of students nationwide were white. An increasing number are coming from poverty-stricken homes. Some are homeless and may live in cars. The families that they come from include divorced parents, merged families, single-parent homes, one or both parents working multiple jobs in order to buy food. Children increasingly are using technology frequently better than their teachers. Existing staff needs to learn the best ways of dealing with these situations. Many children today are disconnected—from school, their family, and society. They are connected instead to social media, cell phones, tablets, and computers. It is fairly difficult for senior experienced staff to adopt and adapt to the new norms.

Older teachers and administrators are very dependable. They have a commitment to their job, and they bring wisdom and experience to the job. They have demonstrated that they have a tremendous work ethic. It is important to treat your senior staff members as if they matter. Because they do. Senior teachers bring a lot of teaching and life experiences into classrooms. Make staff members feel appreciated. Frequently saying thank you for a job well done goes a long way.

What follows is a number of ways to refresh the staff, increasing the likelihood that more of them will remain on the job.

Mentoring

- Senior staff could mentor new staff—and new staff can mentor senior staff. Each group has its own expertise and can learn from one another.

- Extending mentoring beyond two or three years.

- Senior staff can agree to team teach with new people. This can be reciprocated, and then lessons can be organized as to strengths and areas for improvement.

- The superintendent can provide mentoring for principals in the district.

- Principals can hold monthly lunches for staff with ten or more years' experience to tap into their expertise. Use the lunch as a platform for employees to speak their mind freely within the organization. Does your school/district solicit ideas and provide an environment in which people are comfortable providing feedback? If so, employees can offer ideas, feeling free both to criticize and commit to continuous improvement—all factors that contribute to employee retention.

- Ensure that senior staff takes a "stay-in interview" form.

- Establish a Teacher Advisory Committee to allow senior staff to have input into school policy.

Provide Assistance

- Devise and publicize assistance schemes for teachers who need assistance.

- Find ways that senior staff can upgrade their skills by linking the school to businesses that provide training to their staff.

- If possible, create a flexible work schedule for them.

- Provide challenging opportunities. Exemplary teachers want to learn and grow. Unless they can try new opportunities, take on challenging tasks, and attend seminars, they will stagnate. A valued employee must experience growth opportunities within the organization to realize his or her potential.

- Do not take advantage of the hard worker. It is easy to pile work on someone you know is capable of doing it. Make sure that you do not punish someone because you know that the person can do the job.

- Take the relationship beyond the school boundaries. Take time to learn about your senior people—their anniversaries, birthdays, hobbies, movies or TV shows they like.

- Encourage senior members of staff to cooperate. Organize meeting where people can share best practices of dealing with the new student populations.

- Invite members of the new community population to deliver workshops on, for example, Islam, African Americans, and Hispanics. Provide refreshments to staff to make the meetings more palatable.

Continuing Professional Development

- Principals and district officials can provide ongoing professional development to aid existing staff with the tools they need to teach new student ethnicities.

- Ensure that professional development is not only mandatory but free of charge.

- Provide professional development that is close to the schools in order to avoid waste of time and inefficiency.

- Develop partnerships with colleges and universities to provide training to senior staff. Provide college-based professional development in the K–12 schools.

- Organize video-based professional development and make it available to staff in classrooms or to take home and use.

- Organize in-service training as integrated, system-wide, and continuous professional development during the whole of a teacher's career.

- Make a list of what existing staff knows and can teach as well as a list of what they do not know and want to learn.

- Provide training to senior staff in computer skills.

- Pay, if necessary, for teachers' recertification.

Recognition

- Recognize senior staff with recognition awards.

- Provide bonuses at the conclusion of three, five, ten, and twenty years of work.

- Principals can send thank-you notes to senior staff and their families.

- Declare a day off during staff training days.

- Make announcements over the public-address system during the school day so that other staff, students, and parents will be aware of the contributions they have made.

- Make announcements at parent-teacher meetings so that parents are made aware of the retention of senior staff.

- Invite the immediate family of each of those senior staff members who are celebrating three-, five-, ten-, fifteen-, or twenty-year membership to the end-of-semester party.

CHAPTER 6

Additional Strategies to Slow the Educational Exodus

"Modern cynics and skeptics . . . see no harm in paying those to whom they entrust the minds of their children a smaller wage than is paid to those to whom they entrust the care of their plumbing."

—John F. Kennedy

The Value of Education

Assaults on public education have been a part of American history since the beginning. The United States has had a long history of anti-intellectualism. Richard Hofstadter, the author of the Pulitzer Prize–winning book *Anti-Intellectualism in American Life* (1963), has written, "It is ironic that the United States should have been founded by intellectuals, for throughout most of our political history, the intellectual has been either an outsider, a servant or a scapegoat." Society values people who are highly educated, highly trained, and highly experienced—except if they work in education. Why would anyone want to become a teacher? The rewards include low pay, poor working conditions, low social status, having to pay for their own office supplies, and being blamed for not only the educational failures of hundreds of thousands of young people but even the failure to keep America globally competitive. Politicians, the media, and business leaders need to value education and educators. Education is a universal—everyone has had one.

All sorts of people have solutions to educational problems. Reformers have been trying to fix what they perceive to be a "broken system." It has not happened. Gather one hundred diverse people in a room—politicians, business leaders, parents, and the media—and ask them to solve the problems of education, and you will have at least one hundred different responses. These well-meaning people have sound bite solutions to highly complex problems. Mayors have taken over schools in their belief that they can solve educational problems and improve school performance. In most cases, it has not worked. One "solution" is to have non-educators come up with the answers. Imagine having someone become the head of a hospital without any medical experience. Some programs believe that you can take high-performing graduates from universities, train them for five or six weeks, and then put them in a classroom to either sink or swim.

Education and educators are not respected in the United States. According to a report from Education Resource Strategies (ERS), described by Madeline Will for *Education Week*, "The average teacher is not making a living wage." In some states, teachers are eligible to collect welfare. In some locales (for example, San Francisco), teachers cannot afford to live there and must travel well over an hour to get to and from work. According to the ERS, states with low teacher salaries tend to have more teacher shortages, higher teacher turnover rate, and more uncertified and novice teachers than states that pay the most. These are all facts that hurt students, especially those who need good teaching the most. The ERS suggests that states and districts should "front-load" teacher compensation, shifting dollars to the front to keep teachers during their early years, in years four to eight. The low salaries that are paid in those years are compounded by the need for educators to repay their student loans at the same time.

Educators are rebelling against low salaries and poor working conditions, as seen by the strikes in six states in 2018. The shortages of teachers exacerbate the situation as schools struggle to find qualified, licensed people to be in classrooms. Writing again in *Education Week*, Madeline Will reported that according to a U.S. Department of Education national survey, "nearly 1 in 5 public school teachers have second jobs during the school year. Half of teachers with second jobs are working in a field outside of education, while 5 percent of teachers are taking on a second teaching or tutoring job outside of their school districts. . . . Teachers who work a second job earn an average of $5,100 to supplement their incomes." But there is a growing sense of frustration as teachers have to pay not only for school supplies but also for day care for their own children during school hours. Teaching suffers as well, as there is inadequate time to prepare lessons and mark homework. The exhaustion of working two or more jobs makes teachers more susceptible to catching colds and other illnesses. As Madeline Will wrote in her later *Education Week* report, U.S. Department of Labor Statistics survey indicates that teachers are about 30 percent more likely than non-teachers to have a second job. Secondary teachers are more likely to have second jobs than elementary teachers. Male teachers are more likely than female teachers to work outside the school. And a survey conducted by Sam Houston State University in Texas indicates that those who work a second job are more likely to say they are considering leaving teaching.

Not all teacher turnover is a bad thing. Normal attrition is not necessarily undesirable. First, it is inevitable. There are retirements and deaths, as well as teachers and principals moving on. New staff members bring with them fresh young talent, with new ideas, a new vibrancy, a new perspective. But what is happening is an inordinate attrition removing some of the most experienced, most highly trained staff. At the same time, enrollment to become an educator is dramatically down at many of the colleges training people for those jobs.

We need to admit that our current educational system is not operating as well as it should. A student assessment report by the intergovernmental Organisation for Economic Co-operation and Development (OECD) states, "While the U.S. spends more per student than most countries, this does not translate into better performance. For example, the Slovak Republic performs at the same level" as the United States, despite spending less half the money. The report's results rank us as twenty-seventh in mathematics of the thirty-four OECD nations. And in reading and science, the United States is only close to the OECD average. The report adds, There have been "no significant changes" in these performances over time. A broken system requires a radical overhaul and a new cohort of teachers. We face the challenge of a system that needs to improve more rapidly than it has in recent decades. While difficult, it is less daunting than the one imagined by many politicians. The real challenge we face is a system that has not progressed as rapidly as those in other industrialized countries. We have improved, but poverty and disagreements over the goals of education have slowed the pace of reform.

Boosting Wages for Educators

Boosting wages for educators needs to be a part of any solution. According to PayScale.com, the average teacher makes between $27,767 and $48,902, while the average plumber makes between $29,000 and $76,000 per year. The U.S. Air Force values pilots and their skills and knowledge they bring to the job. The cost of a pilot's training and flying experience varies depending on the type of aircraft. A U.S. General Accounting Office report cited the Department of Defense as stating that the cost to train each military pilot through basic flight training is about $1 million, and the cost to fully train a pilot with the requisite operational experience can be more than $9 million. As a result, the Air Force attempts to hold on to as many pilots as possible. It even offers retention bonuses of up to $225,000 for pilots to stay in the service for an additional nine years, as Jennifer Griffin reported on Fox News. How much does it cost our school systems to recruit and train our experienced teachers? Most school systems do not measure the cost of qualified, experienced educators leaving the system or the costs of replacing them. How much is their experience worth? We need to ask, Why do these teachers leave? Maybe then we can find out how to prevent their leaving. Including benefits, teachers are still far behind similarly educated peers, with an 11.1 percent compensation gap, according to a report by the National Conference of State Legislatures. Compounded at 11 percent per year, soon educators are earning half of what others make. Teachers in high-performing countries are compensated more generously than American teachers, typically earning pay like that of other professionals such as engineers and accountants.

Exit-Out or Stay-In Interviews

Many businesses conduct exit-out or stay-in interviews to find out why people are leaving and, if any of those people can be encouraged to stay, what it would take to maintain their employment. School districts and schools could conduct similar interviews to learn why teachers want to leave.

Schools have made major investments in the people they have hired. They normally do not know the cost of those investments if they lose their best employees and then are unable to replace them with the right people. If schools wish to find out why someone is leaving, it is important to conduct an exit interview, as many businesses have learned to do. If several people respond with similar answers, find out if you can fix the problem. Conversely, you might not want to wait until employees are about to leave; instead, proactively conduct a "stay interview" and ask them, "What can I do to remove the barriers to help you do your job better? How can I help you succeed? What do you wish you had known? What do you wish you had been taught?" Schools conducting "stay in interviews" can determine why teachers are leaving by asking them, "What could we have done to keep you in school?"

Exit Interview/Survey

The following example of an exit interview/survey is excerpted from a report written for the SERVE Center at the University of North Carolina at Greensboro by Charles Ahearn, Hobart Harmon, and John R. Sanders.

———

It is our practice to gather information from departing employees. Information you provide will enable the school district to better meet the needs of our teachers, other professional staff, students, and our community. Please answer each item. Your candid responses are very important to us. We treat all information you provide as *strictly confidential*.

1. What grade level(s) did you teach or what position did you hold at the time of leaving our school district?

(Circle all that apply.) Pre-K K 1 2 3 4 5 6 7 8 9 10 11 12 Adult classes

2. How many years did you work in our school district? _____

3. At what school did you teach or what position did you hold?
   _____

4. How many years did you work at a school? _____ At the district level?_____

5. Why did you leave the district? (Check all that apply.)

   ____ Better salary

   ____ Better benefits package

   ____ Better opportunity for professional advancement

   ____ Better parent and community support for student advancement

   ____ Better personal fit with community's culture

   ____ Better social and cultural opportunities in the area

   ____ Better housing available in area

   ____ Better job opportunity for spouse

   ____ Better higher education opportunities for my children

   ____ Better job opportunities for my children

   ____ Pursue advanced education

   ____ More flexible salary schedule with compensation for performance of extra duties

   ____ Fewer instructional demands (e.g., teaching multiple subjects or grade levels)

   ____ Too great an emphasis on teaching to the text

   ____ More reasonable teacher certification standards

___ More supportive superintendent

___ More supportive Board of Education

___ Less scrutiny of my job by parents and community members

___ Less local politics and bureaucracy influencing teacher's effectiveness

___ Dissatisfaction with supervisor

___ Dislike or unsuited for assigned duties

___ Family or personal reasons

___ Health or physical condition

___ Career opportunity in private sector

___ Lack of personal privacy in a small rural community

___ Desire to live in a place more like where I grew up

___ Retirement

___ Relocation

___ Temporary position ended

___ Reduction in force due to downsizing/declining student enrollment

___ Other(specify):_____

6. Please rate your *degree of satisfaction* with the following characteristics while employed in your last position with our school district. For each characteristic, place an "X" in the appropriate column. For any item rated "Very Dissatisfied," briefly explain why in the comments box or in the white space below.

Characteristic	5 Completely Satisfied	4 Very Satisfied	3 Very Well Satisfied	2 Somewhat Satisfied	1 Very Dissatisfied	Comments
District-level leadership and decision making						
School-level administrative support						
Faculty input to decision making						
Curriculum offered to students						
Quality of teaching in this school						
Quality of student counseling in school						
Behavior and discipline of students						
Teacher expectations for student achievement						
Parent involvement to support student achievement / success						

Characteristic	5 Completely Satisfied	4 Very Satisfied	3 Very Well Satisfied	2 Somewhat Satisfied	1 Completely Satisfied	Comments
Community involvement to support student achievement / success						
Classroom facilities and instructional support material						
Professional duties and responsibilities assigned						
Extracurricular duties and responsibilities beyond classroom						
Salary and compensation for position						
Opportunities for profession-al development (continuing education)						
Workplace environment						
Community as place to live						

Stay-In Interviews

Stay-in interviews are one-on-one meetings with between school administrators and high-performing teachers to do three things:

- Reduce teacher turnover

- Lower turnover costs

- Improve retention rates

We could ask high-performing personnel what motivates them to remain in the school or district. It is a way to determine employee satisfaction. Typical questions:

- What do you like about working here?

- What suggestions, if any, would you make about changing your job?

- Do you feel that your work is being recognized?

- What things, if any, would you wish you had known about working here that you did not know?

- What talents of yours are being used? What talents of yours are not being used?

- What would tempt you to leave?

- Will you help us develop a plan to help others want to stay?

- Whom do you look up to at work?

Celebrate Successes

It is easy to become discouraged and disheartened in schools. Educators need to take time to celebrate even "small wins," which lead to bigger wins. In one of my schools, we put up a bulletin board headlined "We don't want to brag but . . . ," announcing to our students, their parents, our staff, and our guests the positives that were happening in our school.

Because we live in a visual society, we posted positive graphs of increased graduation rates and the number of students who were going on to college.

Another morale booster is an electronic sign that read, on a loop, "Through these doors walk the finest people in the world—our students, their parents, our faculty, and our guests."

Principals can recognize incremental successes at the end of the term, in internet posts. Doctors have the right idea by posting their credentials for all to see. Why shouldn't educators proudly list their degrees above the doors to classrooms and offices?

Retirees Need to Be Rehired

States do not like retirees to "double dip"—collecting a pension as well as a salary. Some states, including Oklahoma, have placed a cap on the salary that retired educators can collect. But we have a cadre of experienced educators sitting on the sidelines who are capable of training new people in schools.

Rural Schools

Rural areas face greater problems of teacher retention. Lower salaries than are offered in urban districts, isolation, a shortage of available housing, a lack of professional development, and a shrinking student population all contribute to the problem. According to the National Rural Education Association, rural teachers cite a lack of professional development as a top reason for leaving. In order to improve teacher training, rural schools can use technology such as YouTube videos, with experts in different subjects teaching lessons to supplement the existing staff's instruction. School districts can share their video libraries of the senior experienced staff's teaching lessons to supplement physical instruction. Virtual coaching would also help teachers working in small rural districts or on Native American reservations.

"He who can, does; he who cannot, teaches."

The phrase above was coined by George Bernard Shaw in his play *Man and Superman* (1903). It is indicative of the lack of respect for educators in much of the Western world. I wonder if Mr. Shaw would criticize a list that includes the names Aristotle, Helen Keller, Anne Sullivan, Albert Einstein, Jaime Escalante, Confucius, Mark Twain, Lyndon B. Johnson, J. K. Rowling, Leonard Bernstein, and Laura Bush. What would the world have done without these brilliant individuals who were also educators? Teaching needs to be an honored career that attracts those who could be our most talented teachers and rewards them adequately with pay and respect. Unless that is done, we will continue struggling to fix or remediate problems related to students' interest. Teachers' unions such as the American Federation of Teachers and the National Education Association need to promote education's value to society. Education results in creating all jobs. Companies today—especially today, with the emphasis on technology—would not hire someone lacking an education and a degree to prove it.

Politicians, the media, and business leaders need to value education and educators. Professional educators make the job look easy. People other than educators and their families do not know about the ridiculous and impossible demands being placed on a classroom teacher's time. They believe that the only time a teacher is working is when he or she is in front of a classroom. Parents and grandparents have a difficult time dealing with one, two, or three children for as long as eight hours; imagine being in a room with thirty-four energetic children for that long. Imagine having to plan bathroom breaks around teaching breaks. Imagine working in a non-air-conditioned building in 2018. Today's entry level educator is required to possess and use a wide array of technical knowledge and is expected to be able to make complex and detailed decisions and solve problems at the individual level that take diverse considerations and the ramifications of their actions into account. The days of simply passing tests and having book knowledge are long past. Any implication that "even meeting entry requirements for the Army" should be considered inferior preparation for college or the job market is insulting. Schools are one of the few institutions left in the United States that will train Americans and allow them from all walks of life and all economic levels to succeed. I know there are few outsiders who comprehend the full scope of working in education.

Schools Need to Be Treated as a System

We need to treat the K–12 *system* as a system. It is supposed to operate as one—but it doesn't. Instead, it operates in silos—a K–5 silo, a middle school silo, and a high school silo, followed by a college/university silo. Rarely do these silos interact, meet, or share data, research, or information. We need to change this so that success is built into the system and is not an appendage. If a good person works together with other good people, they will eventually beat a bad system.

Student Teaching

Student teaching should come at the beginning of college, within the first two years, not at the end, so that potential teachers get an early picture of what is expected of them. Fewer of them would leave if they had a real picture of schools and classrooms.

A Globally Competitive School System

We have come to understand that companies such as Amazon, Toyota, Starbucks, and Coca-Cola are no longer simply American but rather are global organizations. America's schools must be globally competitive. That is, the best graduates from New York City's schools are not competing for jobs with the best graduates of schools in Princeton, New Jersey, but with the best graduates from the United Kingdom, Israel, Finland, and Singapore. What can we learn from these top countries and their school systems? Information about countries' teacher policies—how they attract people to the profession, train them, help them improve, and assign them to schools—is available from *Education at a Glance*, published annually by the Organisation for Economic Co-operation and Development (OECD). How do we create world-class, globally competitive schools?

Career and Technical Education

In the past, going to college used to guarantee a more prestigious, higher-paying job. For many of today's college graduates, it merely means grappling with huge outstanding student debt, as well as the possibility of not working in the field for which the graduates have been trained. Some students are capable of working at high-paying jobs by using their hands as well as their head. Some students are frustrated with taking classes that merely prepare them for college. Their boredom leads some to disrupt the learning of others, and teachers have a difficult time dealing with them. We need to hire qualified people to teach career and technical education. These people can be found in a number of different companies. Partnership agreements between schools/districts and local companies would profit both. America needs trained people who work with their hands as well as their brains—for example, carpenters and electricians.

A More Rigorous Recruitment Strategy

We need to institute a more rigorous recruitment strategy. How do we encourage young people to enter the field of education—and once in, keep them there? It takes a very motivated person to meet the physical, emotional, and intellectual challenges of becoming an educator, and if that same motivated individual does the math, looking at the return on investment (ROI), it just does not add up. The federal government can create a "GI Bill" to retain teachers, for example by paying off a percentage of their student loans if they stay in the field for five years. Or the district could pay off a mortgage on a house if the teacher works and lives in a low-performing school district for five years.

Future Educator School Club

There are a variety of school clubs. They function for many different reasons, including providing community service as well as creating and maintaining career interest. These clubs are composed of students with adult advisers. Some of these clubs function at the school, state, or national level. Clubs are frequently started by corporations or political or social organizations. The U.S. Army's Junior Reserve Officer Training Corps (JROTC) is a program offered to high schools that teaches students character education, student achievement, wellness, leadership, and diversity. Some clubs focus on specific career fields and help students understand them better. They include the Future Business Leaders of America, Key Club, National Honor Society, Red Cross, Future Scientists and Engineers of America, and SkillsUSA. The clubs hold competitions and conventions, and present awards, while exposing students to new career opportunities. Some schools already have a Future Teachers of America Club, to provide youngsters in middle and high school with an opportunity to discover more about becoming an educator, as well as the chance to mentor younger students. Students would be recognized with symbols of their participation in the club. Awards could be presented at dinners attended by their parents and other family members. The club could have national sponsors such as the American Federation of Teachers or the National Education Association. Corporations like Google, Apple, Amazon, Microsoft, Facebook, and Twitter might be interested in supporting the organization on a national level. Or foundations like the Bill and Melinda Gates Foundation might be a national sponsor.

Recruit Foreign Teachers

Importing teachers from foreign countries would help fill the gaps of educators in our schools. These foreign teachers could be a short-term solution to our immediate needs to hire foreign language, special education, math, and science teachers. Schools could recruit hundreds of foreign teachers to plug chronic shortages in math and physics departments, a leaked U.S. government memo suggests. The U.S. Department of

Education has launched a program to attract teachers from abroad as schools struggle to recruit locally. Officials could advertise in European Union countries as well as in China and Singapore—both of which are at the top of international league tables for math and science, as Eleanor Harding reported in an article in Britain's *Daily Mail*.

Get the Community Involved

School budgets need to get community support. Yet adults who do not have children or grandchildren in school rarely, if ever, visit a school. Schools could reach out to the community by sponsoring activities that take place in the school. Many student-performed plays have unsold seats. Why not give some tickets to the senior community? Have performances by the school chorus in senior homes or assisted living homes. Invite seniors to present to classes their personal history (in the army, in the war, from work experiences).

When people move to a new area, one of the first questions they ask their real estate broker is "How are your schools?" Look at high-performing, successful communities, and you will find high-performing schools. But because schooling adds to the costs of city or local districts, many communities are building homes without schools. There are gated communities where the signs read, "NO children allowed." Yet who will pay into Social Security and Medicare, for senior citizens to take funds out of if today's students do not pay into the system? It will be difficult getting additional bodies, men or women, into teaching because of low salaries. The National Center for Education Statistics (NCES) produced a table showing that the average salary for public school teachers nationwide in 2008–9 was $53,910, about 2 percent higher than ten years earlier, after adjusting for inflation. Businesspeople measure their success based on two factors: return on investment and value added. The fewer dollars they spend, and more money generated, the greater their profit. Value added equals how much revenue is added with each step in the process. The business community apparently has had a difficult time teaching these concepts to some governors. Current politicians are considering neither return on investment nor value added as they make drastic cuts in education. Apparently their shortsighted, short-term cuts take priority over any long-term thinking. With cuts in education today, the long-term effects will not be felt until the politicians are no longer in office. Besides, the public has long-term memory loss. And the next generation of politicians can always blame the problems they face on their predecessors. It is the ideal win-win situation for today's politicians—and the only losers are the children, their parents, and American society.

Student Loans

Recent reports indicate that the total amount of outstanding student loans in the United States is greater than total credit card debt. Many beginning teachers have as much as $30,000 in outstanding student loan debt. According to The Institute for College Access & Success (TICAS) and its Project on Student Debt, 68 percent of 2015 bachelor's degree recipients graduated with student loan debt, and the average was $30,100 per borrower. Corporations such as Starbucks, Walmart, and McDonald's, in an attempt to hold on to workers, are paying for employees to go to college and get a degree. There is no reason state or local school districts cannot agree to pay off student loans over a three- or five-year period as long as the teacher remains in the district.

Teacher Prep

Colleges prepare educators with a great deal of theory. K–12 educators need more practical information—for example, how to handle classroom management, disruptive students, and students who are attached to their cell phones—as well as theory. State boards of education, in addition to national accreditation groups, should evaluate educator preparation programs that ultimately license teachers. They can use a variety of techniques, including site visits, recruitment efforts, training, hiring, retention, evaluation of graduates' performances in collaboration with districts, and data tracking of teachers after graduation. New Mexico, Tennessee, Delaware, Massachusetts, Louisiana, and Rhode Island are currently doing this.

My mentor Dr. Myron Tribus used this example: "Imagine that you read every book teaching you how to swim. You took all of the tests and passed them all. Then I threw you into the ocean. Would you know how to swim?" Book learning and tests are not sufficient as the sole means of learning. Sometimes, in order to succeed, teachers need to teach.

Yearlong School

School calendars are still based on that of an agrarian society. Students are released from schools so that they are able to plant and harvest. While there is a still a need in agricultural states, the majority of urban school districts can go to a year-round school schedule. Research indicates that "students, especially low-income students without access to enriching activities, stand to lose meaningful knowledge and skills in the eight weeks each year that they're away from instruction," as Cristina Duncan Evans wrote in *Education Week Teacher*. In place of giving students an eight-week break, which produces a summer loss of learning, why not give students three separate shorter breaks? If schools operated all year long with breaks around winter (Thanksgiving through New Year), spring (Easter), and summer for a total of eight weeks, there would be enormous benefits and savings. Professional development could be done during this time, and it would not be limited to one-day training. Teachers would be paid for their additional work time and would undertake prolonged professional development instead of the one-day workshops they presently take. This would eliminate the need to hire substitutes to replace teachers who were attending professional development workshops. It would also eliminate the summer learning loss resulting from the disruption of instruction.

Education's Growing Responsibility

Education has assumed tasks that have been traditionally done by others such as parents and the church. Schools now teach skills that can include swimming, driving, a foreign language, and drug and suicide prevention. It is expected that educators will perform these tasks without additional training or time added to their schedule. More is expected from today's educators. They must prepare students both to thrive in the twenty-first century and to think.

Tenure

Tenure, in the K–12 system, does not mean "a job for life," as many believe. It means that "just cause" is required for discipline up to and including termination, whether the reason is incompetence or extreme misconduct. Tenure was established to protect teachers from being dismissed arbitrarily because of nepotism, favoritism, and or political beliefs. As detailed by Julie Underwood in the journal *Phi Delta Kappan*, some states, including Alaska, Colorado, Connecticut, Delaware, Florida, Illinois, Indiana, Louisiana, Michigan, Nevada, Oklahoma, Rhode Island, Tennessee, Washington, and Wyoming, now require districts to consider performance evaluations in granting tenure to teachers. Some states, including Florida, Idaho, Indiana, Kansas, and North Carolina, have repealed teacher tenure altogether. Idaho's elimination of tenure, however, was reversed by voters. And it means "due process," the right to a fair hearing to contest charges. Tenure does not impede administrators from removing ineffective teachers. Quite simply, any tenured teacher can be fired for a legitimate reason, after school administrators prove their case. Some school districts, governors, and state legislators are intent on replacing higher-paid, senior, more experienced educators with lower-paid teachers in order to save money. Tenure needs to be strengthened, not weakened. The costs of hiring and training new staff do not equal the costs of having experienced, qualified people in classrooms. Teachers are hired on a probationary basis. They achieve tenure by spending three to five years being observed and rated.

Some blame teachers' unions for poor teacher performance. This doesn't make sense. Teachers' unions do not hire teachers.

Highly Qualified versus Highly Experienced

Have you ever had a highly qualified but ineffective teacher—one who knew the material but was not capable of teaching it? We all have. We have all had teachers who had pedagogical information, but they weren't highly effective. We need to have teachers in classrooms who are both highly qualified and highly effective—people who can reach students at all levels. The problem becomes how do we differentiate these individuals? How do we determine their effectiveness? During the time when these people have been hired but have not achieved tenure, they should be observed frequently. Observations can be done by their supervisors or a team of their colleagues. The purpose of these observations should be to improve instruction, not merely to play a game of "gotcha." During this probationary period, they can be let go for any reason whatever. Teachers need to learn the trade of teaching by teaching. Some flounder for a year or two. As Robert Pondiscio, a senior fellow at the Thomas B. Fordham Institute, has said, "Nobody says that to an air traffic controller: 'Everyone crashes a plane their first year; you'll get better.'" No one expects that a child will walk on the first try or that you can easily learn to ride a bike without first using training wheels. Few teachers succeed on their first attempt either.

CHAPTER 7

Creating a Globally Competitive, World-Class School System

"It's too bad that the people who really know how to run this country are busy teaching school."

— A sign in the U.S. Military Academy, West Point, New York

There is a global shortage of teachers. This is being acknowledged by international agencies such as UNESCO, the World Bank, and the Organisation for Economic Co-operation and Development (OECD), as well as the Bill and Melinda Gates Foundation. Newspapers and magazines regularly report on this shortage. The OECD publishes an annual report, *Education at a Glance*, with information about various countries' policies regarding teachers—how they attract people to the profession, train them, help them improve, and assign them to schools.

The populations of most industrialized countries are growing older, with dramatic consequences to economics, politics, and society. America's aging, while substantial, is relatively modest compared to that of many European countries and Japan. Japan's population is aging faster than any other society. According to WorldAtlas.com, 27 percent of the Japanese population is already more than sixty-five years old. This compares to America's 14.9 percent. In the United States, the Social Security Administration estimates that Americans older than sixty-five will constitute 20 percent of the total population by 2030. This means more retirees will be drawing benefits and fewer workers paying taxes. When the seventy-six million baby boomers leave the workforce, today's cohort of students will have to take up the slack. To maintain our nation's productivity in this information and knowledge age, we must educate them with the skills and competencies to do their jobs. An educated workforce will earn more, increasing the tax base, and carry more responsibility, improving our society and economy. But to achieve all this, we must retain today's current teacher population in school, refreshing that population and ensuring that it is adequate to meet the demands of the twenty-first century. Education creates all jobs—especially in the twenty-first century, with its increased emphasis on technology-related employment. No nation, especially in the technological age, can afford to lose teachers and school administrators, who are charged with the responsibilities of teaching and training the next generation. At the same time, the older population is building communities that deny entry to those who are less than fifty-five years old and rejecting school budgets and the building of schools.

Critics of America's schools like to point out that the United States spends more money on education than most other nations. A look by CBS News at one of the OECD annual reports pointed out that the United States spent more, as a share of its economy, than the average country in that survey; in 2010, the United States (at federal and state levels) spent 7.3 percent of its gross domestic product on education, compared with the 6.3 percent average of other OECD countries. (As one form of comparison, noted by Niall McCarthy at *Forbes*, the federal government is spending 3.6 percent of GDP on defense.) We are outspending the average OECD nation, which spent $9,313 per young person. Yet, even though we are spending more dollars, we are not producing better results, as measured by the OECD's PISA and TIMSS examinations.

The Programme for International Student Assessment (PISA) is a worldwide study by the OECD of member and nonmember nations, which evaluates educational systems by measuring to what extent students at the end of compulsory education (generally, at the end of high school) can apply their knowledge to real-life situations and be equipped for society. In 2015, more than half a million students, representing about twenty-nine million fifteen-year-olds in seventy-two countries and economies, took the internationally agreed two-hour test. It was first performed in 2000 and then repeated every three years. Its aim is to provide comparable data with a view to enabling countries to improve their education policies and outcomes. The examination measures reading, mathematics, and science, as well as collaborative problem solving and financial literacy.

The Trends in International Mathematics and Science Study (TIMSS) examination, as described in an overview by the National Center for Education Statistics (NCES), measures trends in math and science achievement. Developed by the International Association for the Evaluation of Educational Achievement (IEA), it is given in sixty-six countries every four years. Yet another international comparative assessment is called the Progress in International Reading Literacy Study (PIRLS), which tests the reading knowledge of fourth-grade students. An NCES overview notes that it was first administered in 2001, and in 2016, about 3,500 to 4,000 students from fifty nations, including the United States, and nearly a dozen other groupings took the examination.

Thinking Globally

We have come to understand that companies such as Amazon, Apple, Toyota, Starbucks, and Coca-Cola are no longer simply American but rather are global organizations. America's schools must be globally competitive. That is, the best graduates from New York City's schools are not competing for jobs with the best graduates of schools in Princeton, New Jersey, but with the best graduates from the United Kingdom, Israel, Finland, and Singapore. When we look to benchmark high-performing schools and students, we look to nearby schools or districts. At best, we look to schools in another state. I believe that we need to benchmark schools in different countries. What do schools in Singapore or in Finland do that we can learn from? What are we doing that we should eliminate? Are there any commonalities in the high-performing nations? In short, how do we create world-class, globally competitive schools?

It is difficult to compare the variety of educational systems, because of differences in culture. Scores change every time the examinations are given; however, there is a consistency in the top rankings. East Asian nations generally score at the top; developing nations in South America and Africa, as well as Arab nations, generally score at the bottom. Based on the results of the 2015 PISA examinations, the highest-performing schools are in

1. Singapore

2. Hong Kong

3. Canada

4. Japan

5. Estonia

6. Finland

7. China

8. South Korea

According to *The Learning Curve*, a report developed by the Economist Intelligence Unit to evaluate data from a multiplicity of sources, the United States ranked seventeenth out of forty nations in overall educational performance.

There are several commonalities in high performing nations:

*   Focus on high-quality teachers

*   Focus on high-quality performance standards

*   High salaries (Estonia being the only exception)

*   Held in high esteem

*   National recognition of the importance of education

Let us take a closer look at features of a few of the high-performing school systems.

Singapore

- Singapore has the youngest teaching staff of the OECD nations. The average teacher's age is thirty-six.

- Singapore has few national resources and therefore has focused on improving its human resources—its population—through education.

- The Ministry of Education selects prospective teachers from the top third of their secondary school graduating class.

- Teachers receive a stipend equal to 60 percent of a teacher's salary while in training and commit to teaching for at least three years.

- As a small country, Singapore has a more centralized educational system. All teachers receive training at the country's National Institute of Education at Nanyang Technological University.

- The Ministry of Education adjusts starting salaries to ensure that teaching is seen as desirable compared to other occupations.

- Professional development is school-based and led by a school's staff developers.

- Teachers are evaluated every year by a number of people using multiple measures.

- Teachers who are highly rated receive bonuses from a school-based fund set up for that purpose.

- After three years of teaching, teachers are assessed to see if they have the potential to move into school leadership.

- As a result of the measures listed above, Singapore does not have a high number of teachers leaving the system.

Finland

A good first-person look at education in Finland is a blog post by Kelly Day, an American who observed the system for months.

- Finland encourages reading at birth by giving parents three books when a child is born—one for the child and one for each parent.

- The requirement to become a teacher in Finland is rigorous. Finland's 62,000 educators are selected from the top 10 percent of the nation's graduates. They are required to possess a master's degree. Teaching is highly competitive because it is a high-paying, prestigious job.

- Students in Finland begin formal schooling at age seven. The children learn by playing and interacting with one another in their classrooms.

- All students in Finland receive free school meals. (In the United States, only low-income students receive free meals.)

- Teachers are trusted to do whatever it takes to educate a child. Goals are not mandated to them. They have input into the goals of each of their classes.

- Teachers spend fewer hours at school each day, and less time in classrooms, than American teachers do. They use the extra time to build curricula and assess their students.

- As noted in an article by Erin Richards in the *Milwaukee Journal Sentinel*, more than 95 percent of teachers in Finland are unionized, paying 1.2 percent of their gross salary to support the Trade Union of Education in Finland, OAJ.

- Parents are provided with three years of maternity leave, along with subsidized day care and preschool for all five-year-olds. In addition, the state subsidizes parents, paying them for every child until he or she turns seventeen years old. Ninety-seven percent of six-year-olds attend public preschool, where children are given some academic education. Schools provide food, medical care, and counseling. Student health care is free.

- A national goal is to mainstream all children. Schools are provided with "positive discrimination" funding to pay for large numbers of immigrants, experts in multicultural learning, special resource teachers, and special needs classes.

- There are no private schools in Finland. All schools are publicly funded. The people running the schools are educators, not career politicians, businesspeople, or military leaders. Every school has the same national goals and draws from the same pool of university-trained educators. Schools are not ranked.

- Students are trained to learn how to learn, not how to take examinations.

- Students in Finland begin school between 9:00 and 9:45 a.m. and end at about 2:45 p.m. (Research indicates that starting school later enhances the learning process, as students are not tired. In the United States, school can begin as early as 7:00 a.m., requiring students, who frequently take a bus to school, to get up as early as 5:00 a.m.)

- Students take fewer subjects and, according to the OECD, have the least amount of homework of any students in the world. The classes are longer but there are fifteen to twenty required breaks during the day. During the break time, students can relax and assess what they have learned. Teachers can also use that time to prepare their next lesson, socialize, or relax.

- In Finland, students are "looped"—they can have the same teacher for up to six years, so that the teacher will become familiar with the strengths and weaknesses of each student. In addition, students develop a bond, with trust and respect for one another and the teacher.

- Schools are small, so that teachers know every student. Nearly 30 percent of Finland's children receive some kind of special help during their first nine years of school.

- The first year of schooling is followed by nine years of compulsory education. Everything after ninth grade is optional, and at the age of sixteen, students and their parents can choose from three categories of further education:

- Upper secondary school, which prepares students for the matriculation test that determines acceptance into a university.

- Vocational education, a three-year program that trains students for various careers but also gives students the option of taking the matriculation examination to enter the university after the program.

- Entry into the workforce. Fewer than 5 percent choose this path.

- The Finnish system does not have standardized testing except for the National Matriculation Examination, which is a voluntary test for students at the end of upper secondary school (the equivalent of America's high school). (By comparison, under the federal No Child Left Behind Act of 2001, scores in frequently given standardized tests are the indicator used to hold American schools and school districts accountable for student achievement.)

Estonia

Estonia shocked most of the world as it moved into the top ten nations in the 2015 PISA exam results. Not only the examination results but also the graduation rate at the secondary level is above the OECD average.

A good first-person source of information about education in Estonia is by Thomas Hatch, in a posting that appears in *International Education News*.

- It is one of the poorest countries among the OECD nations surveyed.

- Teaching is not viewed as a high-status or high-paying occupation, making it difficult to attract people to the field. In fact, according to the OECD, Estonia has the lowest-paid teachers in the world.

- According to a report by Estonian Broadcasting, there are widespread shortages in finding mathematics and science teachers.

- It has the smallest class sizes and teacher-student ratio.

- Many of its schools are in rural areas and have a small student population with low student-teacher ratios.

- Almost 50 percent of Estonian teachers are over the age of fifty. Only 9 percent of teachers are younger than thirty years old. Women make up 82 percent of all teachers.

- Only 14 percent of Estonian teachers think their profession is valued in society.

- Many young teachers leave the profession because they feel that they do not receive administrative support, especially in their early years. They get overloaded and burn out.

The United States

America differs from many of the high-performing countries in a number of ways:

- Our governments (state and federal) do not fund preschool, placing an enormous financial burden on single parents and two working parents.

- According to an article by Niall McCarthy in *Forbes*, the United States has one of the highest rates of childhood poverty. (Israel has the highest, at 28.5 percent. Turkey is second, at 28.4 percent, followed by Mexico, at 25.8 percent. The childhood poverty rate in the United States is 20.5 percent, a little behind Spain's, at 21.7 percent. *Forbes* examined the percentage of children up to seventeen years old living in poverty in selected OECD counties.)

- America has a sharp income inequality.

- America's schools are becoming increasingly diverse ethnically, culturally, and religiously, reflecting the changes in America's population.

- Teaching has become more difficult as more responsibilities traditionally done by parents have been assigned to schools.

- Education and educators are not respected in America. This is clearly shown in the low salaries that are paid. It is compounded by the need for educators to repay their student loans. Teachers in high-performing countries are compensated more generously than American teachers, typically earning pay like that of other professionals such as engineers and accountants.

- Americans feel that the cost of education is expensive—but do not think the same about the cost of incarceration.

- Americans believe that everyone should go to college.

- Vocational education and vocational educators are not valued in American society.

- According to a report by Dr. Richard Ingersoll and others, American educators are getting older—and younger. More teachers are either older or very young and inexperienced.

- America, like most of the rest of the industrialized world, is having difficulty finding a variety of teachers. This gap between what schools need and what colleges of education are producing is especially severe in special education, math, science, and English as a Second Language.

- The average teacher in the United States earns $36,141 per year, according to Alex Caffee at Niche.com.

- According to Dr. Ingersoll, women now represent 77 percent of all educators, increasing in high schools, and will be about 80 percent of the teaching staff by 2020.

- America has had a long tradition of anti-intellectualism, according to noted authors and intellectuals such as Dr. Richard Hofstadter and Isaac Asimov. They described how the foundations of anti-elite, anti-reason, and anti-science attitudes have been infused into America's social and political fabric. Asimov, the science fiction writer and professor of biochemistry at Boston University, wrote, "There is a cult of ignorance in the United States, and there has always been. The strain of anti-intellectualism has been a constant thread winding its way through our political and cultural life, nurtured by the false notion that democracy means that 'my ignorance is just as good as your knowledge.'"

- American education today is losing talented young men and women who are leaving teaching to move into better-paying and less stressful jobs in which they are more appreciated. The past few years have seen an increase in the instability of education, as demonstrated by teachers' strikes in seven states in 2018–2019, including the second-largest educational community, Los Angeles. Increased job satisfaction would result in fewer educators leaving and fewer disruptions like strikes.

- Educators are saddled with high debt because of student loans. In some communities (such as San Francisco), the cost of housing is so high and salaries so low that educators cannot afford to live in the communities where they work. Salaries, especially for starting teachers, are extremely low compared to those for similarly educated people in other jobs. College graduates have incurred large debt paying for college. Average college debt is $25,500. Twenty-nine states and Washington, D.C., require a master's degree. For those with a master's degree, 29 percent had between $29,999 and 79,999 of debt.

- Teachers complain about the lack of input into their jobs.

- America's schools are siloed. There is a K–5 silo, a middle school silo, a high school silo, and a college/university silo. Rarely do these silos interact, meet, or share data, research, or information. We do not have a school system but rather a system of schools.

- The real challenge we face is a system that has not progressed as rapidly as those in other industrialized countries. We have improved, but poverty and disagreements over the goals of education have slowed the pace of reform. We face the challenge of a system that needs to improve more rapidly than it has in recent decades.

- The current school system was created for the workforce we needed one hundred years ago. The current educational process is based on the factory model of the assembly line. This division of labor artificially fragments the learning process.

- America is enamored with everyone going to college. In the past, going to college provided a boost in earnings. This is no longer guaranteed. Some students would do far better if they were prepared to enter the world of work. Students should not need to be prepared for menial jobs that are being phased out by automation.

- We need to hire qualified people to teach career and technical education. America needs trained people who work with their hands as well as their brains, such as carpenters and electricians.

Conclusion

Free public education is a cornerstone of American democracy. Children need good schools with excellent teachers in the classroom and visionary, empowering leaders in the front offices in order to learn properly. Without highly trained teachers and school administrators inspiring potential business leaders, workers, political figures, doctors, lawyers, and entrepreneurs, we will not be able to sustain economic growth.

According to the U.S. Census Bureau in 2018, in projections about the aging U.S. population as described in "2030 Marks Important Demographic Milestones for U.S. Population," "By 2030, all baby boomers will be older than age 65. This will expand the size of the older population so that 1 in every 5 residents will be retirement age. . . . By 2035, there will be 78.0 million people 65 years and older compared to 76.7 million under the age of 18." In other words, the elderly population will outnumber children for the first time in our nation's history—a demographic shift that poses challenges and opportunities to the economy. "The 2030s are projected to be a transformative decade for the U.S. population. The population is expected to grow at a slower pace, age considerably and become more racially and ethnically diverse." Society will become far more dependent on a smaller percentage of our population paying for a larger, aging population with increased health needs, Social Security, and Medicare. All the while, the elderly will be withdrawing larger and larger sums from our national treasury. As our population ages, this will put increasing pressure on our schools to outperform present accepted norms.

The Census Bureau continues: "As the population ages, the ratio of older adults to working-age adults, also known as the old-age dependency ratio, is projected to rise." Schools must do a better job of preparing students to take high-paying jobs. The United States cannot continue to thrive in the twenty-first century without a well-educated, well-trained workforce. which can be achieved only by having a well-paid, well-trained educational staff.

Whenever the everyday burdens of the job get you down; whenever you get depressed; whenever a student, parent, or supervisor picks on you; whenever you forget why you became an educator—I need you to read this poem and remember that this is why you came into the profession.

"The Bridge Builder"

By Will Allen Dromgoole
(1860–1934)

An old man going a lone highway,
Came, at the evening cold and gray,
To a chasm vast and deep and wide,
Through which was flowing a sullen tide.
The old man crossed in the twilight dim,
The sullen stream had no fear for him;
But he turned when safe on the other side
And built a bridge to span the tide.

"Old man," said a fellow pilgrim near,
"You are wasting your strength with building here;
Your journey will end with the ending day,
You never again will pass this way;
You've crossed the chasm, deep and wide,
Why build this bridge at evening tide?"

The builder lifted his old gray head;
"Good friend, in the path I have come," he said,
"There followeth after me to-day
A youth whose feet must pass this way.
This chasm that has been as naught to me

To that fair-haired youth may a pitfall be;
He, too, must cross in the twilight dim;
Good friend, I am building this bridge for him!"

RESOURCES

Articles, Online Postings, Press Releases

Asimov, Isaac. "A Cult of Ignorance." *Newsweek*, January 21, 1980.

Baer, Drake. "37 Billion Is Lost Every Year on These 12 Meeting Mistakes." *Business Insider*, April 9, 2014. https://www.businessinsider.com/37-billion-is-lost-every-year-on-these-meeting-mistakes-2014-4.

Brennan, Imogen. "Australian Teacher Shortage Fears as Student Numbers Soar." ABC News (Australian Broadcasting Corporation), January 18, 2016, updated February 14. https://www.abc.net.au/news/2016-01-18/fears-of-looming-teacher-shortage-as-student-population-soars/7096102.

Burgess, Kim. "Librarians, Assistant Principals to Fill In as Teachers." *Albuquerque Journal*, August 12, 2015. https://www.abqjournal.com/627512/aps-personnel-to-fill-in-as-teachers.html.

Caffee, Alex. "Teacher Salaries in America." Niche.com, updated May 8, 2019. https://www.niche.com/blog/teacher-salaries-in-america/.

Camera, Lauren. "Wanted: Minority Teachers." *U.S. News & World Report*, September 16, 2015. https://www.usnews.com/news/blogs/data-mine/2015/09/16/teacher-workforce-not-diverse-enough-report-shows.

CBS News. "U.S. Education Spending Tops Global List, Study Shows." June 25, 2013. https://www.cbsnews.com/news/us-education-spending-tops-global-list-study-shows/.

Day, Kelly. "11 Ways Finland's Education System Shows Us That 'Less Is More.'" *Filling My Map* (blog), April 15, 2015. https://fillingmymap.com/2015/04/15/11-ways-finlands-education-system-shows-us-that-less-is-more/.

DuFour, Rick, and Becky Burnette. "Pull Out Negativity by Its Roots."

Journal of Staff Development 23, no. 3 (Summer 2002). https://learningforward.org/docs/jsd-summer-2002/burnette233.pdf?sfvrsn=2.

Duhigg, Charles. "Group Study." *New York Times Magazine*, February 28, 2016. https://www.nytimes.com/2016/02/28/magazine/what-google-learned-from-its-quest-to-build-the-perfect-team.html.

Evans, Cristina Duncan. "A Teacher's Case against Summer Vacation." *Education Week Teacher*, July 8, 2014. https://www.edweek.org/tm/articles/2014/07/08/fp-evans-summervacation.html.

Geiger, Abigail. "America's Public School Teachers Are Far Less Racially and Ethnically Diverse Than Their Students." Pew Research Center, Fact Tank, August 27, 2018. http://www.pewresearch.org/fact-tank/2018/08/27/americas-public-school-teachers-are-far-less-racially-and-ethnically-diverse-than-their-students/.

Godsey, Michael. "Why Introverted Teachers Are Burning Out." *Atlantic*, January 25, 2016. https://www.theatlantic.com/education/archive/2016/01/why-introverted-teachers-are-burning-out/425151/.

Griffin, Jennifer. "Air Force, Facing Fighter Pilot Shortage, Offers Retention Bonuses of up to $225,000." Fox News, July 26, 2013. https://www.foxnews.com/politics/air-force-facing-fighter-pilot-shortage-offers-retention-bonuses-of-up-to-225000.

Hackman, Michelle, and Eric Morath. "Teachers Quit Jobs at Highest Rate on Record." *Wall Street Journal*, December 28, 2018. https://www.wsj.com/articles/teachers-quit-jobs-at-highest-rate-on-record-11545993052.

Harding, Eleanor. "Teacher Crisis Is Forcing Us to Recruit Abroad Due to the Shortage of Qualified Staff in the UK." *Daily Mail*, September 5, 2015. http://www.dailymail.co.uk/news/article-3223101/Teacher-crisis-forcing-recruit-abroad-shortage-qualified-staff-UK.html.

Hatch, Thomas. "10 Surprises in the High-Performing Estonian Education System." *International Education News*, August 2, 2017. https://internationalednews.com/2017/08/02/10-surprises-in-the-high-performing-estonian-education-system/.

Heffernan, Virginia. "Meet Is Murder." *New York Times Magazine*, February 28, 2016. https://www.nytimes.com/2016/02/28/magazine/meet-is-murder.html.

Henry, T. "Group to Donate $150 Million to Develop School Leaders." *USA Today*, June 26, 2000.

Higgins, Lori. "In an Already Struggling District, Detroit Schools Deal with Extreme Teacher Shortage." *Detroit Free Press*, May 20, 2017. https://www.freep.com/story/news/education/2017/05/21/teacher-vacancies-detroit-schools/331628001/.

Marsh, Sarah. "Fact or Fiction? The Reason Teachers Choose the Job—and Quit." *Guardian*, October 23, 2015. https://www.theguardian.com/teacher-network/2015/oct/23/fact-or-fiction-the-reasons-teachers-choose-the-job-and-quit. The full report described in the article, *Why Teach?*, is available at http://whyteach.lkmco.org/wp-content/uploads/2015/10/Embargoed-until-Friday-23-October-2015-Why-Teach.pdf.

McCarthy, Niall. "Defense Expenditures of NATO Members Visualized." *Forbes*, July 10, 2018. https://www.forbes.com/sites/niallmccarthy/2018/07/10/defense-expenditure-of-nato-members-visualized-infographic/#4f29628d14cf.

———. "Which Countries Have the Highest Rates of Childhood Poverty?" *Forbes*, January 4, 2016. https://www.forbes.com/sites/niallmccarthy/2016/01/04/which-countries-have-the-highest-rates-of-child-poverty-infographic/#257575841c68. (8)

McKinnon, Merryn. "Teachers Are Leaving the Profession—Here's How to Make Them Stay." Australian National University, January 11, 2016. http://www.anu.edu.au/news/all-news/teachers-are-leaving-the-profession-%E2%80%93-heres-how-to-make-them-stay.

National Center for Education Statistics. "Progress in International Reading Literacy Study (PIRLS)." Overview. https://nces.ed.gov/surveys/pirls/.

————. "Public High School Graduation Rates," updated May 2018. http://nces.ed.gov/programs/coe/indicator_coi.asp.

————. Table 79, "2009 Tables and Figures." *Digest of Education Statistics*, 2009. https://nces.ed.gov/programs/digest/d09/tables/dt09_079.asp.

————. "Trends in International Mathematics and Science Study (TIMSS)." Overview. https://nces.ed.gov/timss/.

National Education Association. "Research Spotlight on Recruiting & Retaining Highly Qualified Teachers." http://www.nea.org/tools/17054.htm, accessed November 28, 2016.

National Rural Education Association. "Tackling the Teacher Shortage in Rural Schools." BetterLesson, April 2, 2018. http://blog.betterlesson.com/blog/2018/04/02/tackling-the-teacher-shortage-in-rural-schools.

Rafati, Shahrzad. "What Steve Jobs Taught Executives about Hiring." *Fortune*, June 9, 2015. http://fortune.com/2015/06/09/shahrzad-rafati-keeping-your-best-employees/.

Richards, Erin. "Union Role Strong in Finland Education." *Milwaukee Journal Sentinel*, November 26, 2011. http://archive.jsonline.com/news/education/union-role-strong-in-finland-education-s536tlj-134546558.html.

Riser-Kositsky, Maya. "Education Statistics: Facts about American Schools." *Education Week*, May 17, 2019. https://www.edweek.org/ew/issues/education-statistics/index.html?cmp=soc-edit-tw.

Sam Houston State University. "SHSU Researcher Measures Teacher Moonlighting, Satisfaction." SHSU News, May 2, 2002. https://www.shsu.edu/~pin_www/T@S/2002/Moonlighting02.html.

Sawchuk, Stephen. "Steep Drops Seen in Teacher-Prep Enrollment Numbers." *Education Week*, October 21, 2014. http://www.edweek.org/ew/articles/2014/10/22/09enroll.h34.html0.

Shinagel, Michael. "The Paradox of Leadership." Harvard Extension School, Professional Development Blog. https://www.extension.harvard.edu/professional-development/blog/paradox-leadership.

Strauss, Valerie. "Why So Many Teachers Leave—and How to Get Them to Stay." *Washington Post,* June 12, 2015. https://www.washingtonpost.com/news/answer-sheet/wp/2015/06/12/why-so-many-teachers-leave-and-how-to-get-them-to-stay/.

"Teacher Shortage Reaching Crisis Levels." *Daily Mail,* September 11, 2014. https://www.dailymail.co.uk/news/article-16644/Teacher-shortage-reaching-crisis-levels.html.

Troy, Forrest J. "The Myth of Our Failed Education System." *School Administrator* 55, no. 8 (September 1998). http://www2.hawaii.edu/~gkellogg/laulima/100/site/readings/frosty_troy.html.

Underwood, Julie. "The State of Teacher Tenure." *Phi Delta Kappan,* March 26, 2018. http://www.kappanonline.org/underwood-state-teacher-tenure/.

U.S. Census Bureau. "2030 Marks Important Demographic Milestones for U.S. Population," revised September 6, 2018. https://www.census.gov/newsroom/press-releases/2018/cb18-41-population-projections.html.

U.S. Department of Education. "U.S. Secretary of Education Arne Duncan Says Colleges of Education Must Improve for Reforms to Succeed," October 22, 2009. https://www.ed.gov/news/press-releases/us-secretary-education-arne-duncan-says-colleges-education-must-improve-reforms-succeed.

Will, Madeline. "Average Teacher Salary Is Below the Living Wage in Half the Country, Report Says." *Education Week,* June 14, 2018. http://blogs.edweek.org/edweek/teacherbeat/2018/06/teacher_salary_living_wage_report.html.

———. "To Make Ends Meet, 1 in 5 Teachers Have Second Jobs." *Education Week,* June 19, 2018. https://www.edweek.org/ew/articles/2018/06/19/to-make-ends-meet-1-in-5.html.

Books

Ackoff, Russell. *The Art of Problem Solving: Accompanied by Aesop's Fables.* New York: John Wiley & Sons, 1978.

Bell, John S., Tony Thacker, and Franklin P. Schargel. *Schools Where Teachers Lead. What Successful Leaders Do.* New York: Routledge, 2013.

Breaux, Annette L., and Harry K. Wong. *New Teacher Induction: How to Train, Support, and Retain New Teachers.* Mountain View, Calif.: Harry K. Wong Publications, 2003.

Collins, Jim. *Good to Great: Why Some Companies Make the Leap . . . and Others Don't.* New York: HarperCollins, 2001. (5)

Covey, Stephen R. *The 7 Habits of Highly Effective People: Powerful Lessons in Personal Change.* New York: Free Press, 1989.

Elmore, Richard. *School Reform from the Inside Out: Policy, Practice, and Performance.* Cambridge, Mass.: Harvard Education Press, 2004.

Hare, Debra, and James L. Heap. *Teacher Recruitment and Retention Strategies in the Midwest: Where Are They and Do They Work?* Naperville, Ill.: North Central Regional Educational Laboratory, 2001.

Hofstadter, Richard. *Anti-Intellectualism in American Life.* New York: Vintage, 1963.

Howard, Lynn F. *Ready for Anything: Supporting New Teachers for Success.* Englewood, Colo.: Advanced Learning Press, 2006.

Jones, Rachel, ed. *Don't Change the Light Bulbs: A Compendium of Expertise from the UK's Most Switched-On Educators.* Bancyfelin, Carmarthen, Wales: Crown House, 2014.

Nisbett, Richard. *Mindware: Tools for Smart Thinking.* New York: Farrar, Straus and Giroux, 2015.

Schargel, Franklin. *Dropout Prevention Tools.* Larchmont, N.Y.: Eye on Education, 2007.

Schargel, Franklin, Tony Thacker, and John S. Bell. *From At-Risk to Academic Excellence: What Successful Leaders Do.* Larchmont, N.Y.: Eye on Education, 2007.

Senge, Peter. *The Fifth Discipline: The Art & Practice of the Learning Organization.* New York: Currency, 1990.

Thacker, Tony, John S. Bell, and Franklin Schargel. *Creating School Cultures That Embrace Learning: What Successful Leaders Do.* Larchmont, N.Y.: Eye on Education, 2007.

Weinzimmer, Laurence G., and Jim McConoughey. *The Wisdom of Failure: How to Learn the Tough Leadership Lessons without Paying the Price.* San Francisco: Jossey-Bass, 2013.

Reports

Ahearn, Charles, Hobart Harmon, and John R. Sanders. *How to Recruit and Retain Teachers and Other School Leaders in Hard-to-Staff Rural and Small School Districts.* SERVE Center at the University of North Carolina at Greensboro, 2006. Exit interview/survey excerpted with permission. https://serve.uncg.edu/wp-content/uploads/2017/09/Rural-RecruitmentToolkit-1.pdf.

Alliance for Excellent Education. *On the Path to Equity: Improving the Effectiveness of Beginning Teachers*, July 2014. https://all4ed.org/wp-content/uploads/2014/07/PathToEquity.pdf.

———. *Teacher Attrition: A Costly Loss to the Nation and to the States*, August 2005. https://all4ed.org/wp-content/uploads/2007/06/TeacherAttrition.pdf.

American Association for Employment in Education. *Educator Supply and Demand Report*, 2015–16. https://www.aaee.org/resources/Documents/2015-16_AAEE_Supply_Demand_Summary.pdf.

Arizona Department of Education Educator Retention and Recruitment Task Force. *Educator Retention and Recruitment Report*, January 2015. http://www.azed.gov/wp-content/uploads/2015/02/err-initial-report-final.pdf.

Australian Senate. *Teaching and Learning—Maximizing Our Investment in Australian Schools*, May 14, 2013. https://www.aph.gov.au/Parliamentary_Business/Committees/Senate/Education_Employment_and_Workplace_Relations/Completed_inquiries/2010-13/teachinglearning/report/index.

Barnes, Gary, Edward Crowe, and Benjamin Schaefer. *The Cost of Teacher Turnover in Five School Districts: A Pilot Study.* Washington,

D.C.: National Commission on Teaching and America's Future, 2007. https://files.eric.ed.gov/fulltext/ED497176.pdf.

Carroll, Thomas G., and Elizabeth Foster. *Who Will Teach? Experience Matters*. Washington, D.C.: National Commission on Teaching and America's Future, 2010.

Darling-Hammond, Linda. *No Dream Denied: A Pledge to America's Children*. Washington, D.C.: National Commission on Teaching and America's Future, 2003.

Economist Intelligence Unit. *The Learning Curve: Education and Skills for Life*. Pearson, 2014. http://www.edmide.gr/anakoinoseis/The-Learning-Curve-Report-2014%20(1).PDF.

Feistritzer, C. Emily, and Charlene K. Haar. *Profile of Teachers in the U.S. 2005*. Washington, D.C.: National Center for Education Information, 2005.

Futernick, Ken. *A Possible Dream: Retaining California Teachers So All Students Learn*. California State University Center for Teacher Quality, 2007. https://www.wested.org/wp-content/uploads/2016/11/139941242532061.TeacherRetention_Futernick07-3.pdf.

Gates, Susan, Jeanne Ringel, Lucrecia Santibañez, Karen Ross, and Catherine Chung. *Who Is Leading Our Schools: An Overview of School Administrators and Their Careers*. Rand, 2003. https://www.rand.org/content/dam/rand/pubs/monograph_reports/MR1679/MR1679.pref.pdf

Hussar, William J. *Predicting the Need for Newly Hired Teachers in the United States to 2008-09*. National Center for Education Statistics, 1999. https://nces.ed.gov/pubs99/1999026.pdf. (1)

Ingersoll, Richard. *Is There Really a Teacher Shortage?* Consortium for Policy Research in Education, University of Pennsylvania Graduate School of Education; Center for the Study of Teaching and Policy, University of Washington, 2003. https://repository.upenn.edu/cgi/viewcontent.cgi?article=1133&context=gse_pubs.

Ingersoll, Richard, Elizabeth Merrill, Daniel Stuckey, and Gregory Collins. *Seven Trends: The Transformation of the Teaching Force*.

Consortium for Policy Research in Education, University
of Pennsylvania Graduate School of Education, updated
October 2018. https://repository.upenn.edu/cgi/viewcontent.
cgi?article=1109&context=cpre_researchreports. (8)

Institute for College Access & Success, The (TICAS). *Student Debt and the
Class of 2015*. Project on Student Debt, 11th Annual Report,
October 2016. https://ticas.org/sites/default/files/pub_files/
classof2015.pdf. (7)

Leithwood, Kenneth, and Carolyn Riehl. *What We Know about Successful
School Leadership*. American Educational Research Association.
Philadelphia: Laboratory for Student Success, Temple
University, 2003.

Leithwood, Kenneth, Karen Seashore Louis, Stephen Anderson,
and Kyla Wahlstrom. *How Leadership Influences Student Learning*.
Wallace Foundation, 2004. https://www.wallacefoundation.org/
knowledge-center/Documents/How-Leadership-Influences-
Student-Learning.pdf.

Levine, Arthur. *Educating School Leaders*. Education Schools Project, 2005.
https://www.nctq.org/nctq/research/1111591043257.pdf.
————. *Educating School Teachers*. Education Schools Project, 2006.
http://edschools.org/pdf/Educating_Teachers_Report.pdf.

MetLife Survey of the American Teacher, 2004–5. https://files.eric.ed.gov/
fulltext/ED488837.pdf.

National Comprehensive Center for Teacher Quality and Public
Agenda. *Working without a Net: How New Teachers from Three
Prominent Alternate Route Programs Describe Their First Year on the Job*,
2007. Issue no. 2 of a series of reports titled *Lessons Learned:
New Teachers Talk about Their Jobs, Challenges and Long-Range Plans*.
https://www.publicagenda.org/files/lessons_learned_2.pdf.

National Council of State Legislatures. *No Time to Lose: How to Build a
World-Class Education System State by State*. November 28, 2017.
http://www.ncsl.org/research/education/no-time-to-lose-how-
to-build-a-world-class-education-system-state-by-state.aspx.

Organisation for Economic Co-operation and Development. *Education *at a Glance*. Annual reports. https://www.oecd.org/education/education-at-a-glance/.

————. *PISA 2015: Results in Focus*. https://www.oecd.org/pisa/pisa-2015-results-in-focus.pdf.

————. *Results from PISA* [Programme for International Student Assessment] *2012*. https://www.oecd.org/unitedstates/PISA-2012-results-US.pdf.

Public Agenda and Learning Point Associates. *Teaching for a Living: How Teachers See the Profession Today*, 2012. https://www.publicagenda.org/pages/teaching-for-a-living.

Stuit, David A., and Thomas M. Smith. *Teacher Turnover in Charter Schools*. Working paper published by the National Center for the Study of Privatization in Education, Teachers College, Columbia University, 2009. https://ncspe.tc.columbia.edu/working-papers/OP183.pdf.

————. *Teacher Turnover in Charter Schools*. National Center on School Choice, Vanderbilt University, 2010. https://www.researchgate.net/publication/255600494_Teacher_Turnover_in_Charter_Schools.

U.S. General Accounting Office. *Military Personnel: Actions Needed to Better Define Pilot Requirements and Promote Retention*. August 1999. https://www.gao.gov/archive/1999/ns99211.pdf.

Acknowledgments

Although my name appears on the cover, many people have contributed to the making of this book.

Starting with the cover, my family collaborated in suggesting the illustration. My family, wife Sandy, sons David and Howard David's wife, Pegi, all made major suggestions which have only made the book better.

I am indebted to Dr. Sandy Addis, Director of the National Dropout Prevention Center for writing the forward.

Several principals contributed to my path and way of thinking: Dr. Irving Anker, Bette Horne, Rae Marcus and Lewis Rappaport, Samuel Forsheit, and William Sigalakis.

Friends and mentors:

Dr. John Bell – Coordinator, EDUCATE/LEAD, Alabama, Alabama Department of Education.

Ed Bales – former Vice President Motorola.

Jean-Claude Brizard – senior advisor and deputy director in the United States Program of the Bill and Melinda Gates Foundation.

Mark Gavoor – Professor at North Park University.

Dr. Tony Thacker – Alabama Assistant State Superintendent of Education.

Wordsmith Richard Slovak who made my words so much stronger, Martha Bullen, publicist, and Deana Riddle, designer.

My thanks to the prepublication readers for their valuable suggestions and insights: Dr. Marie Sobers, Dr. Tony Thacker, Dr Melinda Strickland, Ed Bales, Lori Lamb, and Ann Edenfield Sweet.

About Franklin P. Schargel

Franklin P. Schargel is a former high school classroom teacher, school counselor, and school administrator. His work to dramatically expand parental engagement, increase postsecondary school attendance, and significantly lower his Title 1 high school's dropout rate has gained recognition from the U.S. Department of Education, *Businessweek*, *Fortune*, the *New York Times*, National Public Radio (NPR), and the Public Broadcasting Service (PBS).

In 2014, he was one of only nine nominees worldwide for the Brock International Prize in Education, for "demonstrating clear evidence of success in dropout prevention and for retaining students in alternative education environments." Previously, he received an Individual Crystal Star Award from the National Dropout Prevention Network, and the International Association for Truancy and Dropout Prevention honored him with its Program of the Year Award. He was selected as one of the "Top 30 Education Gurus" for 2015. The following year, Auburn University presented him with its Hero Award, for individuals who have addressed bullying situations in schools or communities through such actions as

- intervening on behalf of bullying victims;
- developing and implementing anti-bullying programs;
- effectively addressing bullying in proactive and unique ways; and
- building partnerships with agencies that share concerns for students' emotional health and safety and that help in interventions through counseling services, sponsorships, programs, etc.

He is the author of twelve best-selling books, one of which has been translated into Spanish and another into Portuguese. His book *Helping Students Graduate*, which utilizes fifteen strategies developed in conjunction with the National Dropout Prevention Center at Clemson University, has been recognized by the U.S. Department of Education as "being effective in solving our school dropout problem." He has also written more than one hundred published articles, including at the Huffington Post, dealing with school reform. In addition, he has spoken at national and international conferences and has delivered workshops and trained educators in forty-nine American states as well as in Latin America and Europe.

For more information, visit his website, www.schargel.com, or search for Franklin Schargel on YouTube.com to view some of his presentations.

Made in the USA
Monee, IL
31 July 2021